Microsoft Access 2013 Essentials

Edward C Jones

Microsoft Access 2013 Essentials

Print edition © 22 January 2015 by Jones-Mack
Technology Services of Charlotte, NC.

Table of Contents

Chapter 1: About Microsoft Access

Welcome to Access, the database management component of Microsoft Office that you can use for various data management tasks. With Microsoft Access 2013 on your computer, the possibilities to create powerful, comprehensive databases are endless. Business tasks that can be readily managed with the help of Microsoft Access include all of the following, and more:

> Bookkeeping: Track the income and expenses of a business

> Sales order entry and fulfillment: Manage and track orders and shipments

> Clients and contacts management: Track client information and provide telephone tickler lists

> Mailing lists: Manage lists of customers and print mailing labels

> Inventory: Track parts or product inventory on hand and generate notices of required reorder status

> Assignment tracking: Track employee assignments, schedules, and progress

This book takes a "get-it-done" approach that is designed to get you up and running quickly utilizing the power of Access. One significant feature of Access is that you can create sophisticated, ready-to-use database applications without being a programmer. You can do so thanks to the database templates that are built into Access and available as a direct download within Access via a connection to the Office.com website. Access also includes a powerful programming language known as Visual Basic for applications, or VBA. While programming is not the topic of this book, it is worth knowing that this capability is there if you need it.

Access is simply phenomenal in its ability to share data with other programs, including Microsoft Office 2013 (Word, Excel, Outlook, and PowerPoint), Microsoft SQL Server, Open Office, Google Docs, Windows SharePoint Server, and many more. Chapter 8 deals specifically with moving data in and out of Access 2013.

Access 2013 is a database manager as well as a database development system. That's a rather complex way of saying it is a tool designed to store information that fits in specific categories, as opposed to information that is free form. A word processor, such as Microsoft Word, stores information as well, but the information is free-form, meaning it follows no particular pattern as you enter your data- a collection of words- as you see fit. With Access, your data falls into specific categories, such as names, addresses, event and meeting times, or student names along with class assignments.

What's new in Access 2013

If you've used Access 2010, you're on very familiar territory with Access 2013. There are actually relatively few changes between Access 2010 and Access 2013. One significant new feature is the ability to build web-based databases with no knowledge of programming. Web-based databases are accessible to users having nothing more than a web browser. (To build web-based databases, you will need your license for Access 2013, and you will also need rights to a Microsoft SharePoint Server.) When you create an Access 2013 web app, you must provide the name of a SharePoint site where the Access database will be stored. You can work with, manage, and uninstall your web app from this SharePoint site just as you would manage any SharePoint app.

A minor change relates to terminology, as far as field types are concerned. Since its inception, Access has used two types of fields for storing text. The two types were formerly known as *text fields*, which store up to 255 characters within any text field inside a single record, and *memo fields*, which store large amounts of text. These two field types still exist, but the names have changed. In Access 2013, what were text fields are now **short text** fields, and memo fields are now referred to as **long text** fields. (The change in naming was made to bring Access in line with its heftier cousin, Microsoft SQL Server.)

Upgrading to Access from the early days (Access 2003 and prior)

If you are moving up to Access 2013 from a very early version of Access such as Access 2003 or earlier, you are in for a lot of change. The user interface, the way things look and operate, has undergone a substantial revision in comparison to the older versions of Access. The old database window has been replaced with a new navigation pane, and a number of menu options and the toolbox have been replaced with the ribbon. The ribbon is organized into groups, and it is *context-sensitive*, meaning that it changes in appearance depending on what task you're trying to accomplish at a given point in time. And a Create tab let you quickly create a new table, query, form, report, macro, or other Access object with just a few mouse clicks. Finally, a template library lets you quickly find and download ready to use databases to meet your specific needs.

About this book

This book has been written to cover all major aspects of Access in a topic-oriented style. You can learn about all aspects of Access by going through the entire book, following the illustrated examples as you go along. Alternatively, you can concentrate on a particular chapter that covers a single area of Access—such as creating reports, or developing complete applications- by reading the particular chapter that applies to your chosen topic.

A note about the illustrations used throughout this book: In many cases, illustrations of full screens within Access have been placed in a landscape format, turned 90 degrees from horizontal. When done, this format was intentional, as the larger view of the image makes for improved readability.

So, you want to manage a database?

It's a fact: in terms of use, the most popular database manager for personal computers is made by Microsoft, but it is not Access. Microsoft Excel is generally used by more people and more businesses as a routine way of storing categorized information than is any other software program on the planet. However, Excel has major limitations when it comes to database management, and Access overcomes those limitations. Also, if you've already stored large amounts of categorized data in Excel and you are running up against Excel's limitations, there are easy ways to move your Excel data into Access

.

What is a Database?

In computer lingo, a *database* is any collection of related information that is grouped together. If you're new to all of this and you are still trying to get your head around the database business, it helps to compare a computerized database to the non-computerized variety. A box of 3-by-5 cards containing names and addresses is a database. A random collection of information is *not* a database. What makes the information a database is the fact that the data is arranged in some sort of logical order. With Access, your data is organized within tables that contain rows and columns of categorized data. One or more tables containing the data in an organized manner is considered to be a database. Access takes this common analogy further by adding the tools that you use to manage the data, such as queries, forms, and reports, and also makes those tools an integral part of the database.

Tables defined

Access stores your data in the form of tables, which are collections of data arranged in rows of records and columns of fields. With this arrangement, commonly used by spreadsheets, each row of the table contains one record, or complete set of information, such as a person in a table of employees or one specific order in a table of customer orders. Each column of the table contains a separate field, or type of information, such as the street address of a person or a dollar amount of a particular sale. The figure that follows shows a small list of names, addresses, and phone numbers of clients of a fictitious company, stored in a table in Access. While for illustrative purposes the figure shown is a small table, you can have tables in Access that literally contain hundreds of thousands of records.

	Client ▾	Last name ▾	First nam ▾	Address ▾	City ▾	State ▾	Zip ▾	Phone ▾
⊞	1	Smith	Linda	101 Main St.	Annapolis	MD	20711	301 555-4032
⊞	2	Johnson	Steven	432 Apple Way	Washington	DC	20005	202 555-3090
⊞	3	O'Malley	Susan	1905 Park Ave.	New York	NY	10014	212 555-7879
⊞	4	Bannnerman	David	434 Ocean Drive	Miami	FL	29101	308 555-2037
*	(New)							

Queries defined

Once your data has been stored in the form of tables, you can obtain specific subsets of that data by using queries. The word "query" literally means to ask, and Access queries provide a way of asking about your data. You can use queries to find a specific record (such as that of a person named Mary Smith), to print mailing labels for all persons living in a certain Zip code, or to display all employees who have not had a performance review in the past 12 months.

Queries let you select and work with data stored in multiple tables. When you design your queries, you'll identify which records should be included in the results of the query, and which fields should be included. You can specify criteria, which determine what records of the underlying table appear in the query. The results of your queries can be used by the forms and reports that you create. Access also lets you create *action queries*, which can be used to quickly modify or delete large amounts of data stored in tables. The following figures show an example of a query's design where the query retrieves data from an employee table, and displays only those records where an employees' job title is 'sales representative.' In the example, the first illustration shows the design of the query, while the second illustration shows the records selected by the query.

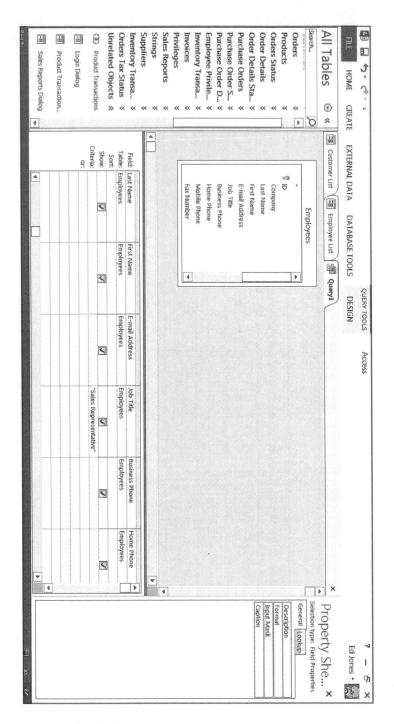

A query's design.

16

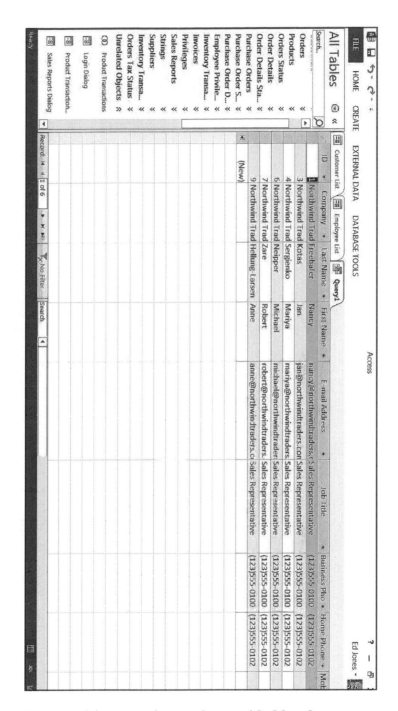

The resulting set of records provided by the query.

Forms defined

In Access, you use forms to display the data that is stored in your tables or queries. If you haven't used forms in a computerized database before, you can think of them as being computerized equivalents of paper based forms that are so familiar to businesses. Forms routinely are used for adding new data to a table and for editing or displaying existing data, usually in a one record at a time format, but occasionally in a spreadsheet-like arrangement. The following figure shows an example of a form in Access.

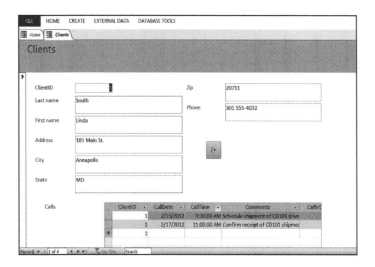

Using the form wizards provided with Access, you can quickly create many variations of forms. Forms can be designed to work with data that comes from more than one table simultaneously. In the above figure, the form shown is based on a relationship between multiple tables, displaying one record from a table of clients along with all detail records showing phone calls made to that client.

18

Reports defined

The desired result of any database is to provide information in the form of reports, and Access is no slouch in this area. You can print reports from tables or from queries, in virtually any desired format. An example of an Access report is shown on the page that follows.

Names and Donations

Last Name	First Name	Member Since	Date	Amount
Askew	Lonnie	3/8/1987	3/18/1993	$25.00
Askew	Lonnie	3/8/1987	2/3/1992	$75.00
Askew	Lonnie	3/8/1987	5/15/1990	$100.00
Askew	Lonnie	3/8/1987	3/22/1988	$50.00
Askew	Lonnie	3/8/1987	3/8/1987	$100.00
Hernandez	Maria	7/21/1989	6/22/1992	$50.00
Hernandez	Maria	7/21/1989	5/16/1990	$40.00
Hernandez	Maria	7/21/1989	7/21/1989	$20.50
Jones	Renee	5/15/1992	4/1/1993	$40.00
Roberts	Norma	3/8/1991	2/12/2012	$50.00

You can design reports manually, or you can use the report wizards to help you quickly design reports. And reports in Access are not limited to mere text; they can also contain graphics, such as photographs of employees, or hyperlinks, such as addresses of websites.

The Access Working Environment

With any new Windows-based software, you learn to make the most effective use of it once you are familiar with the program's main window, and the tools and options contained within that window. Before creating your first objects in Access, it helps to become familiar with the working environment, which includes the *navigation pane*, the *document tabs* bar, the *ribbon*, and the *backstage view.* (The navigation pane, document tabs, and ribbon are highlighted in the figure that follows.)

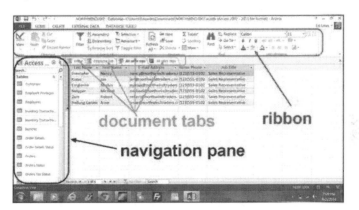

Near the top of the screen is a large area called the *ribbon*. The ribbon contains most of the tools that you will use to perform different Access tasks. The ribbon is *context-sensitive*, meaning, it changes appearance depending on what you're doing at a given time. For example, clicking on the Create tab causes the ribbon to display icons related to creating Access objects, such as new tables, forms, queries, and reports, while clicking on the External Data tab causes the ribbon to show tools related to importing and exporting data. Also note that the ribbon is organized into *groups.* Click the Create tab, and you will see the ribbon change to reveal a group of tools for creating tables, a group for creating queries, a group for creating forms, a group for creating reports, and a group for creating macros and other objects.

At the left side of the screen is an area called the *navigation pane*. This area displays all the different objects in your access database. If you want more space to see your tables and other objects as you work with them, you can alternately hide and re-display the navigation pane by clicking the double-arrow symbol at its upper right.

As you open various Access objects, the open objects also appear on the *document tabs* bar. Click on any object in the document tabs bar to display that object as the active window.

Finally, clicking on the File tab at the upper-left takes you to what is known as *backstage view*. Here, you will find various options for saving, opening, and closing databases, as well as for setting database passwords, changing user permissions when using Access on a network, and printing objects. From this area, you can also open an existing database, create a new database, get information about databases that you already created, or get help using Access from Office.com.

The power of the 'right-click'

For many Access users, the working environment serves as little more than a glorified file manager designed especially for Access- in other words, just a place where you can see the objects in your database. That's a shame, because you can do a lot of work on objects directly from within the working environment by right clicking on various objects and then making a choice from the shortcut menus that appear. For example, right-click on any table that is displayed in the navigation pane. The shortcut menu that appears lets you open the table in design view or as a datasheet, import data into the table, export data from the table to an external file, or rename the table. Or you can right-click a report, and open a shortcut menu that among other things, lets you quickly print a report or display it in print preview mode. The lesson to be learned here is, put that underused mouse button to better use!

Creating Ready-to-Use Databases with Templates

When the entire concept of a relational database makes your head spin, or the type of database that you need serves an everyday task such as keeping a contacts list, managing projects, keeping up with events, or tracking to do tasks, you can quickly create a database that is based upon a *template*. A template is a model that, when opened, creates a complete Access application. In Access, an application is a complete, ready to use database. It already contains all the table relationships, queries, forms, reports, and programming code (known as Visual Basic or VBA code) that is needed to meet your specific tasks. A full installation of Access 2013 includes both web database templates and desktop database templates. The desktop databases are designed to be saved to a shared network location, and multiple users can then simultaneously work with the databases. The web databases are designed to be used with a Microsoft SharePoint server. To create a database that's based on a template, use these steps:

1. On the File tab, click New.
2. In the area near the center of the screen, select one of the sample templates shown (you may need to scroll down to see additional templates). These include ready-to-use databases for the following tasks:
- Assets Tracking
- Charitable Contributions (web-enabled)
- Contacts (web-enabled)
- Events
- Faculty
- Issues Tracking (web-enabled)
- Marketing Projects (web-enabled)
- Projects
- Students
- Tasks

Hint: If you are looking to create a database for a very specific task—say, "real estate listings"-- and you don't see that task listed in the Office.com templates area, you can enter a search term, such as "real estate" in the 'Search Office.com Templates" box. Any templates at the Microsoft Office.com web site matching the search term will be downloaded to your computer. (This assumes you have a live internet connection.)

Hint: Many of the templates at Office.com are not produced by Microsoft, but are instead provided by third party vendors. They appear to be well-designed and clearly had to meet certain quality standards to be included on the Microsoft web site, but Microsoft certainly makes no guarantees that a particular template will accomplish all that you want from the resulting database.

Creating A New Database from Scratch

When you want to create your own database without the aid of any template, just click the 'Blank Desktop Database' button near the center of the screen. Access will create a new, empty database and will assign it a default name, such as Database1, Database2, Database3, and so on. You can and should change this default name to something that is more recognizable later. At the same time, Access will display a table design window in the right portion of the screen, as shown in the following illustration. Access automatically places the cursor in the first empty cell of the first row of the table, as shown here.

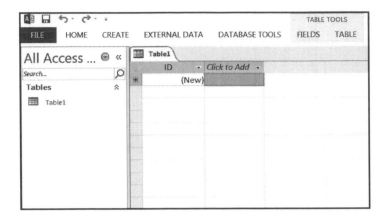

Access does this because the software assumes that, if you are creating a new, blank database from scratch, you will also want to create one or more tables to store your data. However, there are circumstances where this may not be the case For example, you may want to create a new Access database so that you can import a number of lists that you've stored in Microsoft Excel—lists that you probably should have created in Access to begin with!

Once you've created your database, you are ready to begin creating the *tables* that will be used to store the data in your Access database. The ins and outs of Access tables—how to create them, and how to add and edit data to those tables—is the subject of the next chapter.

Summary

In this chapter, you've gotten an overall high-level view of Access. You learned that Access saves your data in a database, and that database contains objects—tables, forms, queries, and reports—that you will use in various ways, to store and manipulate that data. The next chapter will introduce you to Access tables, which are at the heart of any Access database.

Chapter 2: Creating Access Databases and Tables

As mentioned in the previous chapter, Microsoft Access stores your data inside *tables*, and you work with the data using *queries*, *forms,* and *reports.* All four Access 'objects'- tables, queries, forms, and reports- are saved to your Access *database.* In this chapter, In this chapter, you will learn all of the Access essentials about tables, and if you desire, you can follow along with a hands-on example that demonstrates the table creation process.

Tables are at the heart of any Access database, because tables are where all of your data- your categorized information- is stored. In this chapter, you'll learn how to create tables, and how you can add, edit, and delete the data that is in your tables. If you've used Microsoft Excel in the past, you will probably find that Access tables appear very similar to the lists of information that you may have created in Microsoft Excel. But there are some important differences. With Microsoft Excel, the columns of those lists were not necessarily related to any permanent way to each other; in other words, if you had a list of last names in column 'A' and a list of first names in column 'B' of a spreadsheet, and you then sorted column 'A' in order to place the last names in alphabetical order, the first names that were in column

'B' would not necessarily sort, unless you selected them as part of the selection when you did the sort. With Access, you see your data in the form of rows and columns as you do when Excel, but each row is a record, or a complete related set of facts. For example, in a mailing list, a record might contain a last name, first name, street address, city, state, zip code, and perhaps the phone number. If you were to sort any of the columns containing the information in Access, all of the data contained in each record or each row would sort as a complete unit.

In Access, each column is referred to as a *field*, and each row is referred to as a *record*. In Excel, if you wanted to change the name of a column, you would simply rename that column's header. In Access, if you want to change the name of a field, you would actually rename the field while in the design view for the table.

Creating New Tables

In Access, it's a simple process to create new tables, and Access 2013 provides two ways to create a table. One way is by displaying a new table in a datasheet-like format of rows and columns, starting with the first column of an initial row. You begin typing data into the new table. As you type the information, Access automatically determines the field types that should be assigned to each field, based on an analysis of the initial data that you enter into each cell of the datasheet.

With the second method, you first specify the table's design, by identifying the field names and the data types for each field. Once the design is complete, you save the new table, and you can then begin entering data into the table using the data entry techniques specified later in this chapter.

Creating a new table by typing data

To create a table with the 'type in the data' method, click the Create tab of the ribbon, then click the Table icon in the ribbon. A new, blank table appears, and you can begin entering your data in each new field of the table. When you finish entering data in the last field, just click in the first field for the second row of the table, and begin typing your data for the next record. Continue this process until you've completed entering your desired records.

Access automatically creates an autonumber field as the first field in a table, and assigns it a designation as a *primary key*. (You'll learn more about primary keys as well as the 'autonumber' field type shortly.) Access also names the fields *field1, field2, field3,* and so on, with each additional field being assigned a higher number. You can rename the default field names at any time, by opening the table in Design view, and retyping the field names.

Creating a new table by specifying fields and data types

For most users of Microsoft Access, the far more common method of table creation is to tell Access exactly what the table should contain ahead of time, by specifying the field names and the data types before you begin entering any data.

To create a table by specifying the field names and data types prior to any data entry, click the Create tab, then click the Table Design icon in the ribbon. When you do this, a new table opens in Design view, as shown in the figure that follows.

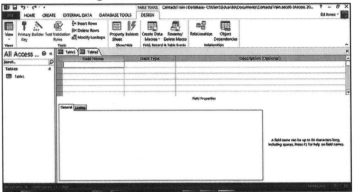

The Table Design window

Access assigns the table a sequential name (such as Table1, Table2, etc.) and that name is visible at the top of the window. When you save the table under a name of your own choosing, this default name is replaced with your chosen name. Whenever you design a table manually, you use this Table Design Window to tell Access the field names and field types used in your table.

In Access, you can examine tables in one of two ways: *Design view*, and *datasheet view*. In Design view, you see the design (or 'layout') of the table. You use Design view to design the *structure* of the table. You name the fields, tell Access what types of data should be stored in the fields, and (optionally) establish any rules that will control data entry as users add data to the table. While in Design view, you can create new tables, or you can modify the design of existing tables.

The other view of tables that you commonly use in Access is called *datasheet view.* Once a new table exists, you can add and edit data in the table, using datasheet view.

While you are in Design view, the upper portion of the Table Design Window is divided into three columns: Field Name, Data Type, and Description. In the Field Name column, enter the desired name for the field. (Your field names can be up to 64 characters in length and you can include letters, numbers, spaces, or punctuation marks.) Since Access allows spaces within field names, you can assign descriptive names to fields. As an example, the name "Date of Vehicle Report" might make more sense to users than a field name of "Veh Rpt Date." However, you should avoid using field names that are overly long, as these can complicate matters when you are trying to design columnar reports. The field names might be so long that it becomes difficult to fit as many columns as you might prefer.

Once you enter a desired field name, press Tab. The insertion pointer will move to the Data Type column. Use the drop-down arrow that appears in this column to choose the desired data type for the data you plan to store in the field. By default, Access assigns all new fields a data type of Short text. You can change this default by clicking the arrow to cause the drop down list box of data types to open, as shown here.

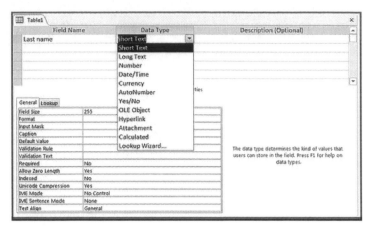

The drop-down list of data types

Access allows a choice of ten types of fields, along with a choice called "Lookup Wizard" which helps you define a field that gets its value by looking up the content of another field in another table. The field types are described as follows:

- Short Text Fields: Use short text fields to store any kinds of textual data, such as customer IDs, part numbers, employee names, and member names and addresses. Short text fields can contain any combination of text and numbers, of up to 255 characters in length. Entries in short text fields can include punctuation marks. Numbers that you don't intend to perform calculations on (such as customer codes, ZIP codes or telephone numbers) should be stored using short text fields. If you need to store very large amounts of text (over 255 characters), use a long text field instead. (Note that in prior versions of Access, short text fields were known as text fields.)

- Number Fields: This type of field stores numbers (other than money), on which you are likely to perform calculations. You can store integers or fractional values (using decimals), and you can enter negative values. You can enter negative values by preceding the value with a minus symbol, or enclosing the value in parenthesis.

- Currency Fields: This field type is a variation of the numeric field, but it is designed to accurately store currency amounts without any rounding errors. By default, numbers that you store in a currency field always maintain a fixed number of digits to the right of the decimal point. (The number of digits is controlled by the currency setting in your Windows Control Panel.)

- Date/Time: Use these for date and/or time entries stored in a table. In Access, validation of existent dates is automatic; you cannot enter invalid dates or times (such as 02/31/12 or 29:68 PM). In many business applications, you will find date/time fields to be useful in calculations, as you can perform date or time-based arithmetic. As an example, you can subtract one date field from another in a report, to include the number of days between both dates within the report.

- Long Text Fields: Use long text fields when you need to store amounts of text that will be too large to fit in a text field. Long Text fields are ideal for information such as item descriptions for sales catalogs, employee job descriptions, article abstracts, or other long paragraphs of text. In Access, long text fields can store up to 32,000 characters. (Note that in prior versions of Access, these were known as memo fields.)

- AutoNumber Fields: This type of field is a self-numbering number field, in which Access automatically inserts sequential values or random values for each record added to the table. By default, sequential integer values are used, and the first record in the table is assigned an AutoNumber value of 1, the next record a value of 2, and so on. (AutoNumber fields are often used as primary keys in relational databases, since they are always unique for every record.) Note that once a record has been added to a table with an AutoNumber field, you cannot change the value assigned by Access in that field. If you delete a record containing an AutoNumber field, the AutoNumber fields in the remaining records are *not* renumbered.

- Yes/No Fields: These are logical fields that contain a Yes/No, True/False, On/Off, or a numeric value of 1 (meaning yes) or 0 (meaning no).

- Hyperlink Fields: You can use Hyperlink fields to store any combination of text and numbers that serves as a web page address, an e-mail address, or as a path of another Access object or to a Microsoft Office document stored on your hard drive or network server.

- OLE Object: You use OLE Object fields to store objects that you create using other Windows applications (such as Microsoft Word or a drawing or paint program). In Windows, an *object* can represent any type of information (a word-processing document, a spreadsheet, or a photo) that can be linked or embedded in Access. The most common use for OLE Object fields in Access tables is to display photos or drawings of people or items, or sound or video clips.

- Attachment Fields: You can use attachment fields to attach any type of file to each record in a table. (As an example, a table of job applicants might include an attachment field named 'Resumes' which you could use to attach Word documents or text files for each applicant's resume.)

TIP: Careful planning will help you to select the most appropriate data type for the fields of your tables. As an example, most fields in a table of names and addresses would usually be short text fields. Numbers that don't need calculations (such as social security numbers, telephone numbers, or ZIP codes) are usually defined as short text fields, even if they contain only numerals. Use the Number data type for numeric amounts with which you plan to perform calculations.

Once you select the desired data type for the field, press Tab again to move to the Description column. In this column, you can enter an optional description of the field. Descriptions may prove helpful for novice users, as they appear in the status bar of a form whenever the insertion pointer is in the field.

Once you enter any desired description for the field, press Tab again, and the insertion pointer will move to the next field. You can continue entering field names, data types, and descriptions for the remaining fields as desired.

Setting Field Properties

During the table design process, you may also wish to set *field properties* for the table. Field properties are settings for the individual fields that let you control how the data is stored or displayed in the table. As an example, if you have a text field that will store social security numbers, you may want to change the field size from the default of 255 characters to something more reasonable (such as 11, for nine numerals and two hyphens). For a number field, you might want to specify the desired number of decimal places. And you also can use the Field Property settings to enter *validation rules*. Validation rules are used to identify conditions that entries must meet before the data will be accepted.

As you are designing a table, you can see the field properties for each field in the table window. When you click anywhere within a particular field, the field properties for that field appear in the lower portion of the Table window, as shown in the following illustration.

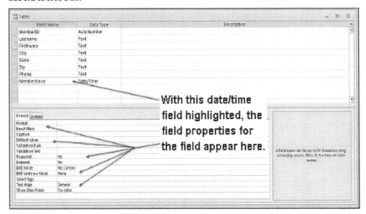

Field properties in a Table window

The properties that Access lets you define depend on what data type is chosen for the field. As an example, with number and currency fields you can specify the desired number of decimal places as a field property. The following table describes the field properties used in Access.

The Field Properties used in Access

Field Size	Specifies the maximum length of a text field, or limits the allowable values in a number field.
New Values	Used only with AutoNumber fields. Determines whether values automatically entered in the field are created in sequential order (the default), or as random values.
Format	Sets a desired format for displaying text, numbers, dates, and times. You can choose from a list of predefined formats, or you can create a custom format using valid formatting symbols.
Decimal Places	Sets the number of places that appear to the right of the decimal point.
Input Mask	Sets a pattern that data entered in the field must match. You can use predefined masks, or you can design your own.
Caption	Sets a default field label that appears as the field name in forms and reports.
Default Value	Specifies a default value that automatically appears in a field when new records are added.
Validation Rule	An expression that defines a data entry rule that the data must meet before it will be accepted.
Validation Short text	Specifies message text that appears if data is entered that

	does not meet the rule specified under Validation Rule.
Required	Determines whether an entry in the field is required for any record added to the table.
Allow Zero Length	Determines whether zero-length (empty) strings are allowed in any record added to the table.
Indexed	Names a single-field index added to speed searches.

Use the following steps to set any of the field properties:

1.   Open the table in Design view, then click anywhere in the desired field.

2.   Click the property you want to set in the lower portion of the window.

2. Enter the desired setting for the property. Or, if an arrow appears at the right of the property, click the arrow and then choose the desired setting from a list of available settings.

Adding a Primary Key

In Access, you can add a *primary key* designation to any field of a table. A *primary key* is one or more fields that uniquely identify every record stored in the table. With primary keys, it is important to note that Access will *not* let you store the same data in the primary key in more than one record. As an example, you would not want to use a "Lastname" field as a primary key; if you were to enter a record in the table with the last name of "Jones," Access would not allow you to enter another record in that table with the same last name.

In Access, you can designate either a single field or a combination of fields as a primary key. Whenever no single field can be used as a unique way to identify a record, you can let Access generate one automatically, by adding an Autonumber field to the table's design and designating that field as the primary key, or you can use a combination of fields as a primary key. For example, a database used in banking might track checking accounts using a combination of bank routing numbers and checking account numbers as a primary key, since no two individual checking accounts would ever have the same routing number and checking account number. You can use the following steps to set a primary key:

1.   While in Design view, click anywhere within the field that you want to use for the primary key. (If you want to assign a primary key based on multiple fields, hold down the Ctrl key and click the field selector to the left of each field you want to include.)

3.   Click the Primary Key button in the ribbon. Access adds a primary key indicator to the left of the fields you've chosen, as shown in the following figure.

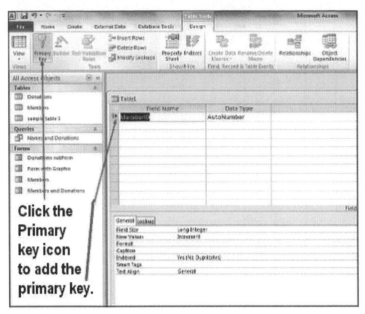

Click the Primary key icon to add the primary key.

The primary key indicator as part of a table's design

Note that unless you are viewing records by means of a *query* (see Chapter 3 for more about queries), Access displays records stored in your table in the order of the primary key. Hence, when there is a specific order you usually want to use when viewing or printing your data, try to design the table so that the primary key keeps the table in the desired order. (If you want to see the records in a different order, you can sort the table on the basis of any field.)

You may notice that when you save the design of a new table, Access will always suggest the use of a primary key if one does not exist. While primary keys are not required, they do speed the performance of Access in sorts, queries, and other common database operations. (A primary key is required when you want to create a default relationship between tables.) Customer numbers, employee numbers, stock numbers, or part numbers are commonly used as primary keys in business use. If a table that you are creating

40

does not appear to need a primary key, you can define a field as an AutoNumber field, name it "Record number" or "Record ID," and let that field serve as the primary key. As data is added, Access will automatically assign the proper values to that field.

Adding a primary key based on an AutoNumber field

If you create a new table in Datasheet view, Access automatically creates a primary key and assigns it the AutoNumber data type. If you are creating the new table using Design view, you can use the following steps to create a primary key based on an Autonumber field.

1. Open the database that you want to modify.
2. In the Navigation Pane, right click the table to which you want to add the primary key and, on the shortcut menu, click Design View. (If you don't see the Navigation Pane, press F11 to display it.)
3. Locate the first available empty row in the table design grid.
4. In the Field Name field, type a name, such as EmployeeID.
5. In the Data Type field, click the drop-down arrow and click AutoNumber.
6. Under Field Properties, in New Values, click Increment if you wish to use incremental numeric values for the primary key (the default), or click Random to use random numbers.
7. Save the changes by clicking the Save icon at the upper left.

41

If the table contains existing data, the new primary key will automatically be populated with data for each existing record of the table.

Rearranging and Deleting Fields

If you decide to make changes to the design of a table, you can easily do so within Access. You can move fields around within a table, you can change the names of fields, you can add new fields, and you can delete any fields that are not needed. To change a field, just click in the field where you want to make the change and make the necessary changes, using the Del or Backspace keys to remove existing characters.

To move a field to another location within the table, first select the field by clicking the Field Selector to the left of the field name. When you do this, the entire field becomes highlighted. Then, click the Field Selector again, hold the mouse button down, and drag the field to the desired location.

If you want to delete a field that is no longer needed, first select the field by clicking the Field Selector. Then, press the Del key, or click the Delete Row button in the ribbon.

To insert a new field at a specific position in the table, click within any row of the table, and choose Edit/Insert Row. A new blank field appears above the existing row, and you can set the field name and type as you would for any field.

Saving the Table

When you have completed the design for a new table, you must save the table structure before you can add data to the table. To save a table, perform these steps:

> 1.   From the menus, choose File/Close or double-click the Control menu icon (it's at the upper-left corner of the Table window). In a moment, you will see a dialog

box asking if you want to save the changes to the table. Click Yes, and the Save As dialog box will appear, as shown here:

The Save As dialog box

2.   Type the desired name for the table. (You can use any names up to 64 characters in length for your tables. You *cannot* use periods, exclamation points, brackets, or leading blanks within table names.

3.   Click OK. If you did not define a primary key for the table, Access will ask if you wish to add one now, by presenting the dialog box shown here.

A dialog box for including a primary key

If you choose Yes, and no AutoNumber field exists in the table, Access will create an AutoNumber field, call it "ID," and make that field a primary key. (If an AutoNumber field already exists, Access will assign a primary key designation to the existing field.) If you click No, Access saves the table structure without a primary key.

Once the table has been saved, it appears by name in the Navigation pane. You can view the table using datasheet view, and you can add, edit, or delete records as desired, as detailed further in the following paragraphs.

Opening an Existing Table

To open the table in Access, double-click on the table's name in the navigation pane at the left side of the screen. The table will open to the right of the navigation pane, and you will see all of the rows (or records) and columns (or fields) within the table. If you need to change the information that's stored in a particular field of an existing record, all you need to do is to click within that field and select the data and delete it and type the new information, or use your normal editing keys along with the backspace key and make corrections as necessary.

Entering Data

If you want to enter a new record, simply click in the first field of the first empty row of the table, and begin typing your information. You can use the tab key to move out of one field and into the next field as you enter the data. When you reach the last field in a table and enter data, pressing the tab key once more will move you to the first field of the next new record, and you can enter additional records using the same technique.

Adding data to long text fields

You can try to enter data directly into a long text field while you are in datasheet view, but usually it is impossible to see all of the data at once. You can easily remedy this problem by pressing Shift+F2 while the insertion pointer is inside a long text field.

This action opens a Zoom box in the field, so that you can see the data while you work with it.

After making your entries or edits in the Zoom box, click on OK to accept the changes.

Adding data to OLE object fields

As mentioned earlier in this chapter, you can specify OLE object as the field type in an Access table. OLE object fields are used to store OLE data, such as word processing documents, spreadsheets, or sound or video clips. When you need to insert OLE data into an OLE object field, follow these steps:

1. In the Windows application that contains the data you want to insert into the Access field, select the desired data.

2. Using the menu options of that Windows application, choose Copy to copy the desired data into Windows clipboard memory.

3. Switch to Access, and place the insertion pointer inside the OLE object field of the desired record.

4. Right-click and choose Paste from the pop-up menu that appears in order to place the OLE data into the field.

TIP: If the OLE object that you want to insert exists on your computer's hard drive, (such as music or video files), another way to add them to an OLE object field is right-click on the OLE Object field, and choose Insert Object from the shortcut menu that appears. Doing so brings up an Object Type dialog box, shown here.

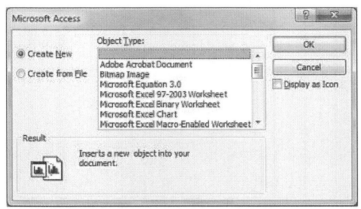

You can choose Create New in the dialog box to create a new object of the type selected in the list portion of the dialog box. Or you can choose 'Create from File' and browse to the file location of the object where you can select it and click OK to store the OLE object in the field.

Adding Attachments to an Attachment Field

To attach a file to an attachment field, simply double-click on the paper clip that you see within the Attachment field. When you do so, a file dialog box will open, and you can navigate to the file location of the file to be attached, select the file, and click OK.

Moving Around Within a Table

As for navigation while you are doing a large number of edits, you can use the up and down arrow keys to navigate between records. And you can use the page up and page down keys to quickly scroll between a large number of records in a table. However, if the table contains hundreds or even thousands of records, using the arrow keys or the PgUp and PgDn keys is going to be unworkable. In such cases, you can use the Navigation Bar, or you can search for the record using the Find option.

The Navigation Bar appears at the very bottom of the table window, and looks like this:

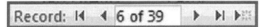

You can use the < and > buttons to move to the prior or next record, or use the |< and >| buttons to move to thee first or last record in a table. And you can click within the numeric portion of the bar- where the current record is indicated by means of a numeric value, such as "record 6 of 39" in this example, and you can type another value and press the Enter key. For example, if your table contained 2,405 records and you know that the record that you want to edit is around number 2,300, just click in the numeric area, type 2300 and press the Enter key to jump to that record.

There are also a number of shortcut key combinations that you are certain to find useful when navigating within a table. These are listed here for your reference.

Home- moves to the first field in the current record

End- moves to the last field in the current record

CTRL plus HOME- moves to the first field in the first record

CTRL plus END- moves to the last field in the last record

Tab, right arrow, or Enter- moves to the next field

Shift plus Tab- moves to the prior field

Up arrow-moves up one row or one line in text boxes containing multiple lines

Down arrow- moves down one row or one line in text boxes containing multiple lines

PgUp- moves up one page, or when at the beginning of a record, moves to the top of the preceding record

PgDn- moves down one page, or when at the end of a record, moves to the top of the next record

Searching for Data with Find

With very large tables, you are likely to find that the most efficient way to locate a specific record for editing is to perform a search, using the Find option. First, click anywhere within the field that you want to search. Then in the home tab of the ribbon bar, click Find (It's the icon that resembles a large pair of binoculars).When you do so, the Find dialog appears, shown here:

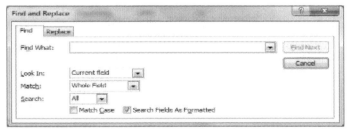

In the Find What box, enter all or part of the term you want to search for. In the Look In box, leave the

option set to Current Field if you want to search just
that field, or change the option to 'Current Document'
if you want to search the entire table (with large
tables, this can be slower). And if you are searching
on a partial string of text, change the 'Match' option to
'Any part of field.' (The default, Whole Field, finds a
match only if your entry matches the entire field.)
When you've finished selecting the desired Search
options, click the 'Find Next' button in the dialog box
to search for the first matching occurrence of the term
in your table. If there are more records containing the
search term, you can repeatedly click the 'Find Next'
button to move to each matching occurrence until you
locate the desired record.

Using find and replace

If you have a large number of edits to perform as a
single operation, such as replacing the word
"grommet" with the words "rubber washer" in a table
of 3000 plus entries in a hardware inventory database,
you can use the find and replace option to perform this
type of task quickly. On the Home tab in the ribbon
area, click the Replace icon (it's located just to the
right of the 'Find' binoculars). This will bring up a
Replace dialog that's very similar in appearance to the
Find dialog box. The appearance of the Replace
dialog box is shown below:

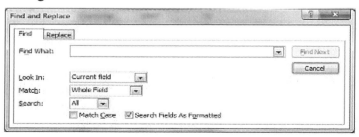

As with the Find dialog box, enter all or part of the term you want to search for in the 'Find What' box. In the Look In box, leave the option set to Current Field if you want to search just that field, or change the option to 'Current Document' if you want to search the entire table (with large tables, this can be slower). And if you are searching on a partial string of text, change the 'Match' option to 'Any part of field.' After entering the information about the term you want to find, click the "Replace' tab of the same dialog box, to reveal the following dialog box:

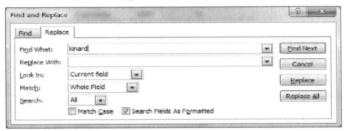

In the 'Replace With' portion of the text box, enter the replacement text. You can then click 'Replace' to replace just the first occurrence of the text, or you can click 'Replace All' to replace all occurrences of the word.

Deleting a record

If you want to delete an entire record, first select it by clicking the *record selector*—that's the square box to the far left of the entire record. Doing so will select that record, causing it to appear highlighted. You can then click the Delete icon on the Home tab, or you can simply press the DEL key. (**Note** that it may not be a wise idea to delete records that exist in a table, because there may be a relationship between that table and other tables in your database. For example, if your database has a table of contacts and a table of

50

phone calls made to each contact, chances are a relationship exists between the contacts table and the calls table. If you delete a record for a particular contact, and phone calls have already been entered for that contact in the calls table, there is now no way to identify exactly who those calls belong to. But if you are deleting a record that you have just entered for the first time, normally this won't cause any problems.)

Saving your data

Once you make corrections to a particular field in one record of the table, you can save your changes by clicking the Save icon at the upper left. But if you are making a large number of corrections, or if you are entering a large number of new records, you don't necessarily have to do anything as you go along to save the data. Unlike Excel, Access will automatically save your data as soon as you move off of a particular record. It's always a wise idea to use the Save icon to save the last record that you are working on before closing a table.

Customizing the display of the table

If you do a significant amount of work with your tables in Datasheet view, you will probably want a way to change the appearance of the data to suit your preferences. You can change the width of columns, change the height of rows, move columns to new locations, and even change the fonts used to view the data.

To change a column width: place the insertion pointer over the right edge of the top of the column until it changes to a double headed arrow, then click and drag the column to the desired width.

To change the row height: place the insertion pointer at the far left edge of the table between any of the new record selectors until it changes into a double headed vertical arrow. Click and drag the row to the desired height.

To move a column to another location: first, select the column you want to move by clicking its field selector at the top of the column. Then click the column and drag it to its new location.

To hide or show a column: right click the column's header (the name of the field), and in the pop-up menu that appears, choose 'Hide Field.' And if you've hidden fields and you want to see those fields again, just right click on any of the column names, and choose 'Unhide Fields' from the pop-up menu. A dialog box containing a list of all hidden fields will appear, and you can select the field that you want to unhide from the dialog box.

You can easily change the fonts used by the text in your tables by selecting the options in the text formatting area of the ribbon, as shown here.

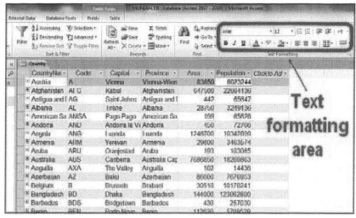

Text formatting area

You can choose fonts by name, a desired font size, whether to apply bolding or italics to the entire table, or even choose your choice of background colors. And you can click the text formatting drop-down at the bottom of the text formatting area of the ribbon, to reveal the datasheet formatting dialog box, shown here.

Here, you can choose from a variety of options, such as whether your tables appear with a flat or sunken look, whether horizontal or vertical grid lines appear, and even the line styles that will be used for your borders and for your grid lines. Selections that you make here are stored to the database, and apply just to the currently active table. Take the time to experiment with these various options, until you find a table layout that is most comfortable for your use.

A Hands-On Example: Creating an Access Table
*Beginning in this chapter you will see various hands-on examples that are designed to quickly demonstrate the features of Access. **Whenever you see text appear using this different font, it means that you should be doing something, and for best results, you'll want to grab your keyboard and follow along.***

If you haven't already done so, launch Access now. Depending on your operating system, you may need to open the Start menu and look for Microsoft Access (all versions of Windows prior to Windows 8) or look in your Apps panel and double-click the Microsoft Access icon (Windows 8 only). When Access starts, you will see the Access welcome screen, shown here:

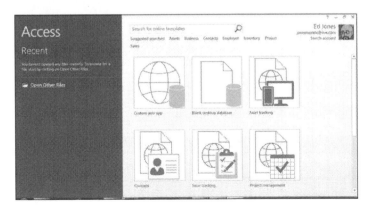

Hands-On: Creating the database

The database you create in this example contains one table, which will be used to record names, phone numbers, and other details of the sales contacts. To create the database and the required table, performed the following steps:

Click the Blank Desktop Database button in the center of the screen. Access will display a blank desktop database prompt for a name as shown here.

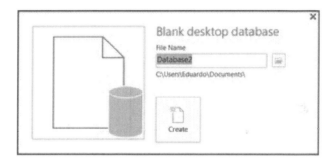

You should change this default name to something that is more recognizable now, so—

Click in the File Name field and type **ContactsTrain,** *then click the* **Create** *button.*

ContactsTrain is the name that we've suggested for this training database; feel free to give it a different name if you prefer, as long as you can find your database on your particular system when it's time to open the database and follow along!

Because you have just created a new, empty database, Access assumes that you also wish to create at least one table to store your data. Access will display a table design window in the right portion of the screen, as shown in the following illustration. Access automatically places the cursor in the first empty cell of the first row of the table, as shown here.

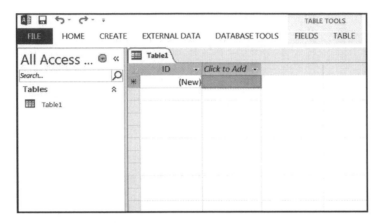

Access 2013 provides two ways to create a table. One way is by displaying a new table in a datasheet-like format of rows and columns, starting with the first column of an initial row. You begin typing data into the new table. As you type the information, Access automatically determines the field types that should be assigned to each field, based on an analysis of the initial data that you enter into each cell of the datasheet.

With the second method, you first specify the table's design, by identifying the field names and the data types for each field. Once the design is complete, you save the new table, and you can then begin entering data into the table using the data entry techniques specified later in this chapter. You will use this second method of table creation in the hands-on exercise that follows.

*In the Menu bar, click the **Create** tab. Then in the Ribbon area, click the Table Design icon.* When you do this, the Table Design window appears.

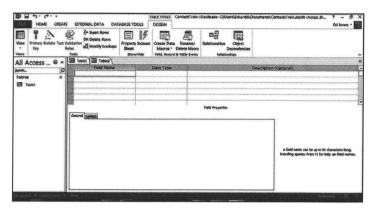

The upper portion of the Table Design Window is divided into three columns: Field Name, Data Type, and Description. In the Field Name column, you will enter the desired names for the fields of your table. (Your field names can be up to 64 characters in length and you can include letters, numbers, spaces, or punctuation marks.) Since Access allows spaces within field names, you can assign descriptive names to fields. As an example, the name "Date of Vehicle Report" might make more sense visually than a field name of "Veh Rpt Date." However, you should avoid using field names that are overly long, as these can complicate matters when you are trying to design columnar reports. The field names might be so long that it becomes difficult to fit as many columns as you might prefer.

With the cursor flashing in the first field name column, enter Contact ID as the first field name, and then press the Tab key to move cursor to the Data Type column.

In the Data Type column, press the letter 'A' to change the field type from short text (the default) to AutoNumber. In this type of field, Access stores a numeric value that is automatically incremented for each new record that is stored in the table. You can click the arrow at the right side of the column to open a menu showing your choices of field types: the choices include autonumber, short text, number, date/time, currency, long text, yes/no, hyperlink, OLE object, attachment, calculated, and look up wizard. (Note that what were called **text fields** in prior versions of Access are now referred to as **short text fields**, and what were **memo fields** in prior versions are now referred to as **long text fields**.)

Press the Tab key twice to move past the description column (descriptions are optional) and back to the field name column for the next field.

Enter the remaining field names and data types shown in the table below. To select each data type, click on the arrow at the right side of the data type column, and choose the desired field type from the menu that appears.

Field name	Data type
Last name	Short Text
First name	Short Text
Company	Short Text
Address	Short Text

City	Short Text
State	Short Text
Zip code	Short Text
Phone	Short Text
Fax	Short Text
Last contact	Date/time
Comments	Long Text

Click anywhere in the first field (titled contact ID), and click the primary key button in the ribbon area near the top of the screen to make this field a primary key. At this point, your table structure should resemble the example shown in the illustration on the following page.

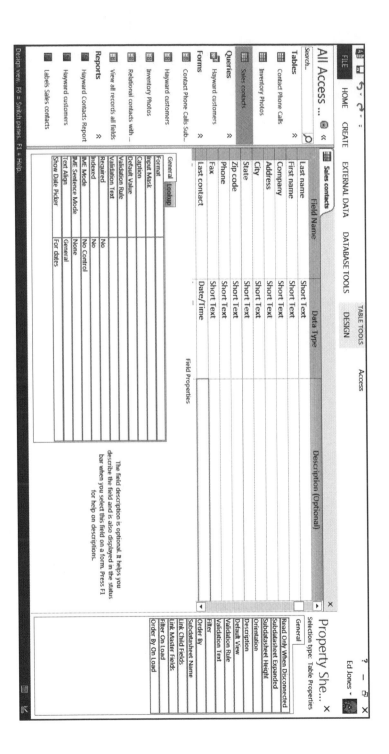

60

Click the Save icon (it's the graphic of a disk) above the menu bar, or at the left side of the screen, click File and choose Save. When asked for a table name, enter 'Sales contacts.'

Press Ctrl+F4 to close the table design window. The new table, sales contacts, now appears in the navigation pane at the far left, under 'All Access Objects.' At this point, both the database and that table exist; you could, if desired, create additional tables and store them in this database. For this example, only one table is needed; however, you can have over 32,000 database tables in any single database.

In our example, for some fields that will store numbers (such as zip code and phone fields), we suggested text fields as the data type rather than number fields. In Access, you should only use number fields when you intend to perform calculations on the contents of those fields; otherwise, use short text fields (which can store letters, numbers, or a combination of both.)

Once the table has been saved, it appears by name in the Navigation pane. You can view the table using datasheet view, and you can add, edit, or delete records as desired, as detailed further in the following paragraphs.

Hands-On: Opening an Existing Table

To open the table in Access, double-click on the table's name in the navigation pane at the left side of the screen. The table will open to the right of the navigation pane, as shown on the following page.

FILE | HOME | CREATE | EXTERNAL DATA | DATABASE TOOLS | FIELDS | TABLE

TABLE TOOLS

Ed Jones

All Access ...

Search...

Tables
- Contact Phone Calls
- Inventory Photos
- Sales contacts

Queries
- Hayward customers

Forms
- Contact Phone Calls Sub...
- Hayward customers
- Inventory Photos
- Relational contacts with ...
- View all records all fields

Reports
- Hayward Contacts Report
- Hayward customers
- Labels Sales contacts

Sales contacts

Contact ID	Last name	First name	Company	Address	City	State	Zip code	Phone
1	Johnson	Mary	Acme Fibers, Inc	1700 La Costa R	Hayward	CA	94542	408 555-2320
2	Benson	Terry	Swift Technolog	2100 Stanford S	Santa Monica	CA	90404	301 555-2000
3	Alvarez	Maria	Image Systems,	9090 Telstar Dri	El Monte	CA	91731	818 555-4050
4	O'Malley	Sandy	Corporate Supp	1111 Lincoln Ave	Hayward	CA	94545	510 555-2985
5	Richardson	Linda	Richardson Pres	234 Tacoma Wa	Seattle	WA	98101	206 555-4787
6	Abrams	Aaron	Abrams Supply C	1919 Fairway Dr	Seattle	WA	98102	206 555-9876
(New)								

Record: 1 of 6 | No Filter | Search

Once the table opens, you will see all of the rows (or records) and columns (or fields) within the table. If you need to change the information that's stored in a particular field of an existing record, all you need to do is to click within that field and select the data and delete it and type the new information, or use your normal editing keys along with the backspace key and make corrections as necessary.

Hands-On: Entering Data

If you want to enter a new record, simply click in the first field of the first empty row of the table, and begin typing your information. You can use the Tab key to move out of one field and into the next field as you enter the data. When you reach the last field in a table and enter data, pressing the Tab key once more will move you to the first field of the next new record, and you can enter additional records using the same technique.

Before you can experiment with queries and reports, you will need to add data to the table that you created. In the Navigation pane at the left side of the screen, right-click the Sales Contacts table that you just created and choose Open from the menu that appears. Using the TAB key to move from field to field, enter the following new record: You can simply press TAB to move past the ContactID field and into the Last Name field, and Access will automatically place the next successive available value within the autonumber field.

```
Johnson
Mary
Acme Fibers, INC.
1700 La Costa Mesa Drive
Hayward
CA
94542
408 555-2330
408 555-2358
9/22/2012 0:00:00
Expressed high level of interest in our
Premier line of #10 envelopes.
```

*After entering the entry in the Comments field,
press TAB again, and the cursor moves to the
first field of a new, blank record. Press TAB once
more, to move past the autonumber field and into
the Lastname field. Enter the five additional
records that follow, using the same techniques
that you used for the first record: (Few people are
fans of mundane data entry tasks, but we
suggest that you take the time to do this, as
these records will be used in the remaining
hands-on exercises throughout this text.)*

```
Benson
Terry
Swift Technology
2100 Stanford St.
Santa Monica
CA
90404
301 555-2000
301 555-2020
9/25/2012 0:00:00
Wants full pricing information on our
Standard line of 10 envelopes.
```

Alvarez
Maria
Image Systems, Ltd
9090 Telstar Drive
El Monte
CA
91731
818 555-4050
818 555-4868
9/23/2012 0:00:00
Wants to know current discount on bulk
cartridge orders.

O'Malley
Sandy
Corporate Support
1111 Lincoln Ave.
Hayward
CA
94545
510 555-2985
510 555-3121
10/02/2012 0:00:00
Did not need pricing info we sent on
Standard line envelopes. Is interested in
pricing on interoffice mail envelope.

Richardson
Linda
Richardson Press
234 Tacoma Way
Seattle
WA
98102
206 555-4787
206 555-4789
10/05/12
New customer, interested in entire
product line.

```
Abrams
Aaron
Abrams Supply Co.
1919 Fairway Drive
Seattle
WA
98102
206 555-9876
206 555-9877
9/27/12
Weekend call with urgent request for a
sudden client job. Need follow-up.
```

When you finish entering the data, note that you don't have to take any action to save the data. Access saves your data as you move the cursor off each record.

This completes the Hands-On Example which has provided you with a real-world experience with creating an Access database and adding new tables. You can save and close the database, if you wish, as it will be referred to in other hands-on exercises in successive chapters.

Establishing Relationships Between Tables

One of the most powerful features of Access is the ability to establish relationships between multiple tables. You can establish relationships in Access using the Relationships icon on the Database Tools tab of the ribbon. After you establish relationships in Access, the relationship is automatically used to link fields in the queries, forms, and reports that you create. Although you're not required to establish relationships between tables, this feature saves time and ensures proper end results when you are designing complex forms and reports.

Another advantage of the establishment of relationships between tables is that it allows for the use of *referential integrity,* which requires relationships between tables to work. Referential integrity is a method Access uses to automatically protect data against certain changes or deletions which would break the links between records in related tables.

Part of the process of designing tables for Access applications involves the selection of an appropriate field or combination of fields to be used as the primary key within the table. A primary key is a field or combination of fields that serves to uniquely identify every record within a table. While Access does not require the addition of a primary key to any table, one is necessary to establish a relationship between the table and another (related) table.

Entire books have been written on the subject of relational database planning and we won't belabor the point here. But suffice to say that if you plan to create moderately complex databases using Access, you should be familiar with the various types of relationships that can be created. Access (along with nearly all database managers used by personal computers) supports three types of relationships: one-to-one, one to-many, and many-to-many. The terms refer to the number of records found in the initial, or "parent" table that can be related to the number of records found in the related, or "child" table.

For example, consider the simple case of the database containing two tables, one of customers of a small supply company, and another table of phone calls made to each of the customers. This example demonstrates the one-to-many relationship, commonly found in most database applications. In this example, the Customers table contains the names, addresses, and phone numbers of various customers of a sales organization. A second table, Calls, contains a listing of all phone calls made to a particular customer. Each record in the Customers table (which represents a single customer) can be related to one or more records in the Calls table. The result is a one-to-many relationship between the Customers table and the Calls table. And in this example, the relationship between the tables is based on the CustomerID field, which is a primary key in the Customers table, and a foreign key in the Calls table. Since no two customers can have the same CustomerID number, the CustomerID field uniquely identifies every customer in the Customers table. In this example, since one customer can have any number of phone calls made to that customer, a one-to-many relationship exists between the Customers table and the Calls table. This is by far the most common type of relationship you will need in your Access applications.

Less commonly, you will encounter one-to-one and many-to-many relationships. In a one-to-one relationship, one record in a table is related to one (and only one) record in another table. An example of this type of relationship can commonly be found in the design of personnel tracking databases, where employee medical coverage is typically tracked in a table separate from employee office locations. One table may contain the office location and phone extension for an employee, and another table may contain the health provider name and the annual cost of the medical plan for which the employee is a subscriber. Each table will contain one record for a given employee, and the tables will be linked on a common field (such as an employee ID number or a social security number). In this case, a one-to-one relationship exists between the tables.

Also less common than the one-to-many relationship (and by nature more complex) is the many-to-many relationship. In this type of relationship, one or more records in one table are related to one or more records in another table. A common example (often used to teach the basics of database design) involves classes and students at any college. A database designed to track classes and students at a small college could have a table named Classes, and a table named Students. A record within the Classes table representing any single class would be related to a number of students; correspondingly, a record within the Students table representing a particular student would be related to any number of classes. In such a case, a many-to-many relationship exists between the Students table and the Classes table, because any one class will contain a number of students, and any one student will be enrolled in a number of classes. Access does not directly support the creation of this type of relationship, but it can be implemented with the use of an intermediate, or "linking" table between the two tables containing the "many" records.

As mentioned earlier, you can establish relationships at the database level to support the design of your relational queries, forms, and reports. You do so by means of the Relationship Tools area of the ribbon. Once you establish relationships in Access, the relationships are automatically used to link fields in any queries, forms, and reports that include multiple tables within their design. While you aren't required to use this feature to establish relationships (you can just design relational queries instead), it can be a significant time-saver, as it simplifies the design of any relational forms or reports within your application.

The second advantage of establishing relationships between tables in Access is that it enables the use of *referential integrity*. As mentioned earlier, referential integrity is a process by which Access automatically protects the data within your related tables from certain changes or deletions that would break the relationship between records. For example, with referential integrity enabled, you could not delete a given Customer from the Customers table in the example described previously without deleting all the corresponding calls for that Customer. And Access would not allow you to add a record to the Calls table containing a CustomerID number that does not exist in the Customers table. In Access, you can see any relationships that have been established at the database level in the Relationships window, an example of which appears later in this chapter. To view this window, click the Database Tools tab, then click the Relationship icon in the ribbon bar.

In any database that you may be working with, you can establish relationships at the database level with these steps:

1. With all tables visible in the Navigation Pane, click the Relationships icon on the Database Tools tab of the ribbon. When establishing relationships at the

database level for the first time, an empty window appears with the Show Table dialog box, shown here.

The Show Tables dialog box

2. In the Show Tables dialog box, click the Tables tab to see all tables in the database, or click the Queries tab to see all queries in the database. To see both tables and queries simultaneously, click the Both tab.

3. Select the table or query that you want to add to the relationship, and click the Add button. (Alternately, you can just double-click the desired table or query.)

4. Repeat step 3 for every table or query that is to be added to the Relationships window. (The order in which the tables or queries is selected does not matter.) When done, click Close.

5. Next, create the links between the common fields of the tables (or queries) that form the relationships, by dragging the field from the primary table (or query) to the matching field of the related table (or query). When you drag and drop a field, the Edit Relationships dialog box appears, as shown here.

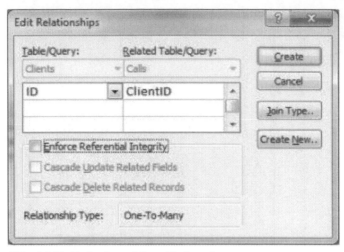

The Edit Relationships dialog box

6. If necessary, you can change the fields that Access suggests in the Edit Relationships dialog box as the basis for the link between the related tables or queries. Access makes its best guess as to the proper field and that guess is generally, but not always, correct. While fields used to link tables do not need to have the same name, they must be of the same type, with the exception of AutoNumber fields which can be linked to Number fields.)

7. If you wish to enable referential integrity, turn on the Enforce Referential Integrity check box. With the check box turned on, you can also enable the Cascade Update Related Fields and Cascade Delete Related Fields options, if desired. (With Cascade Update Related Fields turned on, any changes made to a primary key of the parent table or query are automatically updated in the foreign key fields for all related records in the child table or query. With Cascade Delete Related Records turned on, if a record is deleted in the parent table or query, all related

records matching that record's primary key in the child table are automatically deleted.)

8. If the relationship type shown at the bottom of the Edit Relationships dialog box is not the type that you prefer, click the Join Type button to display the Join Properties dialog box, shown in the next illustration. In this dialog box, you can select the desired type of join (one to one or one to many) by clicking the desired option. In most cases, you will want a one to many relationship. When done, click Close to put away this dialog box

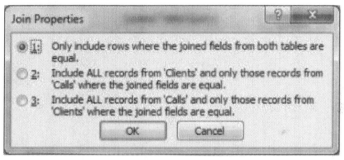

The Join Properties dialog box

9. Click the Create button in the Edit Relationships dialog box to create the relationship. When you do this, a line appears between the tables indicating the type of relationship that exists between the tables, where the numeral "1" indicates a "one" side and the infinity symbol indicates a "many" side.

10. Repeat steps 5-9 for every relationship that you want to add between tables (or queries), and close the Relationships window. When Access asks if you wish to save the changes to the Relationships window, click Yes.

In some cases, relationships can appear quite complex, depending on the number of tables and the overall level of complexity of your application. An excellent example of this is the Northwind Traders 2007 sample database that can be downloaded for free at Office.com. The database contains numerous related tables. The following figure shows the Relationships window for the Northwind Traders database.

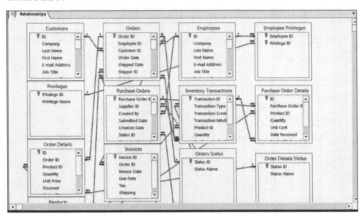

The Relationships window for the Northwind Traders database

If the process of normalizing the design of a database (eliminating redundant data and choosing appropriate relationships) is new to you, Access offers help in the form of the Table Analyzer Wizard. The Table Analyzer Wizard analyzes your existing tables (they must contain data), and makes recommendations as to how your data can be properly split into multiple tables. For this analysis to work correctly, the table must contain at least three records of actual data.

To start the wizard, click the Database Tools icon in the ribbon, then click Analyze Table. After clicking Next twice to bypass explanatory screens about how the Table Analyzer works, you will be asked to select the table that the wizard should split into multiple related tables, as shown in the following figure.

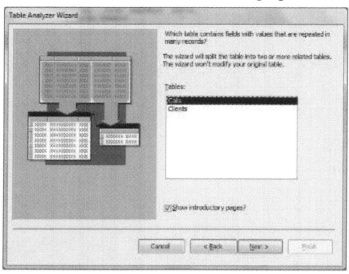

The Table Analyzer Wizard dialog box

Once you select the desired table, you can then choose whether you want the wizard to make decisions for you, or whether you just want to see suggestions that you can later use to manually split the table. If you allow the wizard to decide and you don't care for the results, you can use the Back button to go back and make your own decision as to where the table should be split.

Summary

In this chapter, you learned the details behind the creation of tables, which serve as the heart of your Access database. You learned how to create new tables, how to add, edit, and delete data in your tables, and how to make the most of relationships between tables. In the next chapter, you'll learn how you can obtain specific data from your tables by creating *queries* that retrieve desired data.

Chapter 3 - Creating and Using Access Queries

In the previous chapter, you learned how you can create tables, the foundation of data storage, in Access. You learned how to open and edit tables in datasheet view, how to organize your tables by means of primary keys, how to search for data, and how to establish relationships between tables. In this chapter, you'll learn how you can put an important feature of Access- *queries*- to use in your databases. Access uses a technology known as *graphical query by example* to let you graphically describe the data that you want to retrieve. Queries are the Access objects that you use to obtain the precise data that you need from your tables, and to supply that data to your forms and reports. And the query by example technology built into Access allows you to design queries by dragging objects around within a query design window.

In Access, most queries that you will create are known as *select queries.* They are appropriately named because you use them to select the information you need (such as all records relating to a particular customer, or all employees who work out of the New York office and live in New Jersey or Connecticut). You can use select queries to show all records in a table sorted in a certain order, or just a subset of records meeting a certain criteria. You can include all the fields of a table, or only selected fields. And you can even use queries to display selected parts of records from more than one table. You can also use queries to sort your records, and to perform calculations based on number or date fields. Queries are commonly used as a source of data for reports, and you can use them to supply selective data to forms. The figures on the following two pages show an example of a query's design, and of the resulting table produced by the query.

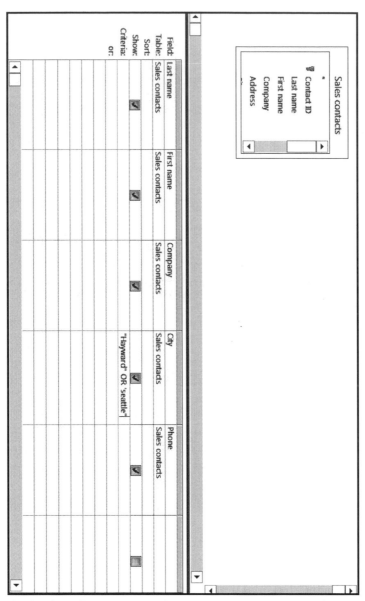

A design for a query that selects customers in Hayward or Seattle

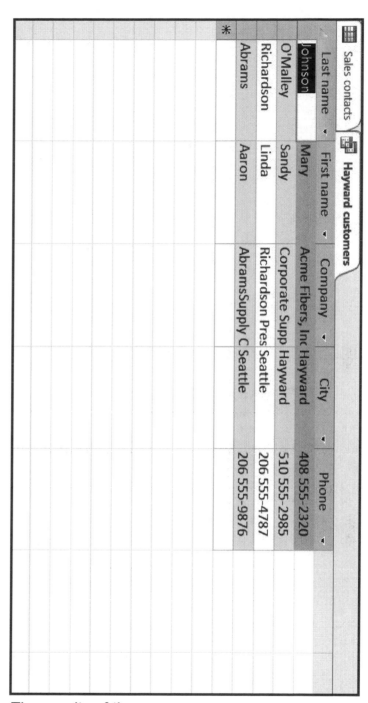

The results of the query

When you run a select query, the data appears in a window called a *dynaset*. In appearance, a dynaset resembles a table, but in reality it is a *dynamic* set of records drawn from the table or tables that the query is based on- hence its' name, dynaset. In a dynaset, Access displays the actual underlying data as it provides the answer to the query. Therefore, if you edit the data in the dynaset, you are changing the data in the original table or tables. An advantage to the use of Access by multiple users on a network is that, since the data is dynamic, changes made by others to the same tables will be immediately apparent.

Select queries are just one type of query offered by Access. The other type of query that you will commonly use is the *action query*. Action queries perform a prescribed action (make changes) to a group of records. You can use action queries to change a group of records en masse, to delete a group of records, or to copy a group of records into a new table. As an example, if you needed to change the area code for an entire group of customers located in a particular city in one operation, you would use an action query to do this.

A third type of query that is not commonly used (but nevertheless is available when needed) is the *crosstab* query. You can use crosstab queries to summarize numeric data in a crosstab, spreadsheet-like format.

Queries as a Data Source

If you already possess some experience using Access, you may be accustomed to using query-by-example as a way to generate ad hoc listings of data that meets a certain criteria. However, it is important to realize that in Access, queries can do much more than this. Access queries can be saved as a part of your database, and in their saved form, you can use them as a source of data for forms and reports. This feature of Access can save you significant amounts of time when you need a database that can be used by everyone in the office, and you don't have the time (or desire) to train the entire office staff on the details of using Access. Let's take an example: perhaps you are using a database that contains a large listing of sales, and you need a report that shows all sales of a particular customer. Using Access, you could create a query that retrieves all the sales for that customer, and save the design of the query. You could then base a report on that particular query. And if you later changed the query's design to retrieve all the sales for a different customer, the report when reprinted would automatically contain the sales for that new customer. A significant advantage to designing your forms and reports to use queries as a data source is that whenever you open the form or reprint the report, the query runs automatically, and you see the most up-to-date data in the form or report. You can base your forms or reports on queries by choosing the query by name in the dialog box that appears when you initially create the form or report. Existing forms and reports can be based on queries by setting the Record Source property for the form or the report to the name of the query. For specifics on how to do this, see Chapter 4 (for forms) or Chapter 5 (for reports).

Creating a Query

Access lets you create queries using either of two methods. You can create queries manually, or you can use a feature known as the *query wizards*. The query wizards are designed to help you quickly create queries for special tasks, such as displaying duplicate records, finding records that lack matching records in another table, or creating numeric crosstabs. But for many common database needs, you will want to design your own queries manually. This may sound

81

challenging, but it is actually a fairly straightforward process. In the ribbon area you click the Create tab than you click the Query Design option. You then add the fields you want included in the query to the query design. In the Sort row, you specify any sorting conditions for the data. And finally, in the Criteria row, you enter *expressions* to ask any questions about the data so that the records you desire are retrieved by the query.

Once you have finished designing the query, you can save it as a part of the database. At a later time, you can run the query to retrieve your desired data. To create a new query manually, you use these steps:

1.   In the ribbon area, click the Create tab.

2.   Click Query Design. A new query appears in the lower portion of the window, and the Show Table dialog box appears above the window, as shown in the following figure.

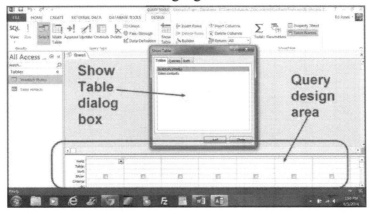

The Design Query window with the Show Table dialog box

In the Show Table dialog box, you can click the Tables tab to view only tables, the Queries tab to view only existing queries, or the Both tab to view both tables and queries. Next, click the table or query that should act as a source of data for the new query. After selecting the desired table or query, click Add, and a list box of the fields appears in the Query window. (If you are designing a relational query to draw data from multiple tables, you must repeat this step for all tables needed in the query.) When you are done adding tables to the query, click Close to close the Show Table dialog box.

The Query window is made up of two parts. The upper portion contains the field lists for all tables (or existing queries) that you included as data sources in the query. The lower portion displays the *query grid*, where you indicate which fields should be included in the query, how records should be sorted, and the criteria that will select the desired records from the tables.

Adding Fields to the Query

Once you have chosen the source of the data for the query, you need to tell Access which fields need to be included in the results of the query. The most commonly-used method of adding fields to the query is to click and drag each desired field from the Field List to the next empty cell of the Field Row in the query grid.

Alternately, you can double-click any field in the Field List, to add it to the next blank column in the Field Row of the query grid.

> **TIP:** If you want to quickly add all the fields in the Field List to a query's design, double-click the Title Bar at the top of the Field List, to highlight all of the fields. Then click and drag any of the highlighted fields to the first empty cell in the Field Row of the query grid. The fields will move as a group.

The following figure shows an example of a query based on a table of countries of the world, along with their population statistics. In this case, the query uses a single data source- a table named Country (as seen

83

in the upper left portion of the design window). In the Query Grid portion of the window, you can see the Country, Code, Capital, Province, Area, and Population fields have all been added to the query design. Looking at the Sort row of the Query Grid, you can see that the query will sort the records based on the Country field, in ascending order. Finally, in the Criteria row, the value **> 100000000** tells Access to display only those countries with a population in excess of 100 million inhabitants.

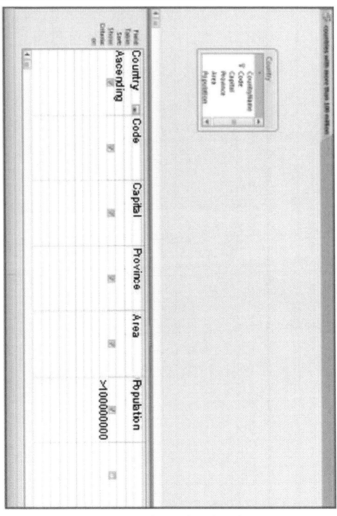

An example of the design of a simple query

Rearranging, Inserting, and Deleting Fields

As you are working with a query, you can rearrange the fields in the query grid, and you can add new fields or remove existing fields. To move a field, click the *field selector* (the narrow bar directly above the field name) to highlight it. Then, click the selector again and drag the column to the desired position in the grid. To insert a field, first click inside the Field List to select the field that you wish to insert, then drag that field from the Field List to the desired column in the query grid. (Any existing fields will move to the right to make room for the new field.) To delete a field, first click the field selector in the query grid to select the field to be deleted, then press the Del key.

Specifying Sorting and Selection Criteria

The last step in designing the query is to specify how the data should be sorted, and what *criteria* (or 'selection rules') should be used to retrieve the necessary data. To specify a sort order, use these steps:

1. Select the field that Access should assign the highest priority to when ordering the records. As an example, if you are querying a table of customers, you may want to see the records in order of customer number.

2. Click in the Sort row for the field that you want Access to assign the highest priority for the sort. Then from the drop-down list, choose the desired sort order (ascending or descending).

3. If you are sorting based on multiple fields, repeat the above steps for each additional field that you want to sort. (When you are sorting based on more than one field, the field of highest priority must be the leftmost field in the query grid. If

needed, you can click and drag columns to different locations in the grid so that the highest priority field for the sort is the leftmost field.)

To specify a selection criteria that determines which records should be retrieved, use these steps:

1.   Click in the Criteria row inside the field that you want to use to retrieve the needed information.

2.   Enter the selection criteria in the column, If you want to retrieve all records where a given field contains a certain value (such as a date, or a numeric value), enter that value. If you want to retrieve all records matching a certain text string, such as a City field equal to "Dallas", enter that text string.

3.   Repeat Step 2 for all additional fields where you need to specify selection criteria.

Running the Query

Once you have performed all of the above steps, you can run the query by choosing View>Datasheet View at the far left of the ribbon, or by clicking the Run button in the ribbon (it's the icon resembling a large exclamation point). Using either method, the desired data appears in a dynaset looking very much like the rows (records) and columns (fields) of any Access table.

Using Criteria

The real power behind the effective use of queries in Access lies in properly designing your criteria expressions in order to retrieve the precise data you need. With queries and criteria, actual examples best demonstrate the effective use of criteria. Hence, this portion of the chapter will illustrate how you can design various select queries using the Northwind Traders 2007 database that can be downloaded from

Office.com and installed from within Access. If you want to follow along and you don't have this database on your machine, you can use these steps to quickly install this database:

1. Open Microsoft Access.
2. On the New tab (which appears by default when you start Access), enter **Northwind** into the 'Search for templates' search box.
3. When 'Northwind 2007 Sample Database' appears in your search results, click to select it.
4. When prompted, enter a filename for your Northwind database in the Filename box.
5. Click the Create button.

Access will download the Northwind database from Microsoft (which may take a while, depending on the speed of your internet connection), and the database will open automatically when it has been installed on your computer.

Open the Northwind Traders example database. You will be prompted to login with a fictitious employee name; for the purposes of this example you can select any employee name and click the 'Login' button.) Try these steps to demonstrate the use of criteria in Access queries.

1.   Click the Create tab in the ribbon, then click Query Design.

2.   In the Show Tables dialog box that appears over the Query Design window, click Customers, then Add, then Close. The resultant query contains the Field List for the Customers table.

3.   Double-click the Title Bar at the top of the Field List to highlight all the fields, then click and drag any of the highlighted fields to the Field row of the query grid, underneath the first empty

column. This causes all fields in the Fields List to be added to the query grid.

4.   In the grid, turn off the check boxes for the e-mail address, home phone, and mobile phone fields. (Since these fields are empty in the sample Northwind database, we'll omit them from the view.)

5.   For this example, you want to see all customers in Boston, so use the scroll bar (if necessary) to scroll the query grid until the City field comes into view. Then click in the City field within the Criteria row, and type **Boston**. (If you move out of the field, Access will automatically surround the entry with quotation marks, indicating that it is a text value.)

6.   On the Home tab, open the View drop-down and choose Datasheet View. The dynaset that appears shows the records for those customers based in Boston, as shown in the figure on the following page.

ID	Company	Last Name	First Name	Job Title	Business Pho	Fax Number	Address	City
2	Company B	Gratacos Solsor	Antonio	Owner	(123)555-0100	(123)555-0101	123 2nd Street	Boston
18	Company R	Autier Miconi	Catherine	Purchasing Representativ	(123)555-0100	(123)555-0101	456 18th Street	Boston
*	(New)							

7. Choose View/Query Design to switch back from the dynaset to design view for the query.

If you needed to see all records meeting a certain criteria in two or more fields, you would simply enter the desired criteria in each field of the query grid. For example, to see all purchasing managers based in Memphis, TN, you would perform these steps:

1. In the Criteria row inside the City field, replace the previous entry of "Boston" with **Memphis**.

2. Click in the Job Title field within the Criteria row, and enter **Purchasing manager**.

3. Click the Run button in the ribbon. The dynaset that appears when you do so shows the records for those purchasing managers based in Memphis.

4. Choose View/Query Design to switch back from the dynaset to design view for the query.

When you enter criteria into the Criteria row of a query grid, you are entering *expressions* that define conditions the data must meet before it will be included in the results of the query. As an example, entering **San Diego** in a Criteria row underneath a City column would cause Access to retrieve only those records containing the words "San Diego" in the City field of a table. If a table of items for sale contained a Price field, you could enter **>15 and <20** in a Criteria row underneath the Price column of a query to cause Access to retrieve only those records with amounts between $15.00 and $20.00 in the Price field of the table.

When you need to specify more than one condition for a query, you can do so using either of two methods. You can enter the desired conditions in multiple columns of the query grid, or you can include OR statements as part of the expressions that you enter. For example, in a table of employees for a company with multiple offices in different cities, you could enter **Johnson** in the Criteria row underneath the Last Name column, and you could enter **New York** in the Criteria row underneath the City column. This would cause Access to retrieve all records containing the name "Johnson" in the Last Name field, and "New York" in the City field of the underlying table. Alternately, you could enter **San Diego** in the first criteria row underneath the City column, and **San Francisco** in the second criteria row underneath the City column. This would cause Access to retrieve records with either the phrase "San Diego" or "San Francisco" in the City field of the underlying table.

The secret to effective design of select queries involves constructing your expressions properly, to obtain the data that you need. While the examples cited in this chapter have been relatively simple, you can use operators to build very complex expressions for your query criteria. Operators that are commonly used include the math operators (such as >, <, >=, <=, <>) and the logical operators, such as And, Or, and Not. Table 3-1 provides examples of typical criteria that are commonly used in creating queries.

Table 3-1

Field	Criteria expression	results of criteria
City	"Dallas"	records containing Dallas in the city field
City	"Dallas" or "Houston"	records containing Dallas or Houston in the city field

City	NOT "Chicago"	records containing any entry except Chicago in the city field
Last Name	Like "G*"	records containing last names that begin with the letter G
Last Name	Like "[A-M]*"	records containing last names that begin with any letters from A to M
Last Name	Like "Th*"	records containing last names that begin with the letters "Th"
Price	< = 22.50	records containing amounts of 22.50 or less in the Price field
Price	between 35.00 and 80.00	records containing amounts from 35.00 to 80.00 in the Price field
Date Sold	< Date( ) - 90	Sales older than 90 days old
Date Sold	Year([When Sold]) = 2011	Sales in calendar year 2011

Building Queries Based on OR Criteria

Until now, the examples provided in this chapter have described queries that retrieve records based on one criteria "and" another criteria being true. Since both criteria must be true, the type of criteria used is known as AND logic. Another type of criteria that you will often need is referred to as OR logic. In this case, the records are retrieved if one criteria "OR" another criteria evaluates as true. Here's a real-world example, again using the Customers table in the Northwind Traders database. Assuming you need to retrieve all records for customers based in Boston or Seattle, using such "OR" logic in Access is a simple matter. You add the additional criteria on multiple lines below the first criteria, using as many lines as are needed. As an example, consider the query shown here.

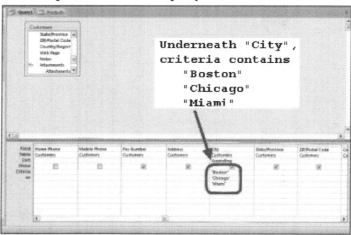

An example of a query using OR logic

In this example, expressions have been entered in three Criteria rows underneath the City field. Because the entries are Boston, Chicago, and Miami, the query will retrieve only those records where the entries in the City field is either Boston, Chicago, or Miami.

Combining AND & OR Criteria

Often, you will find it necessary to mix the use of "AND" and "OR" criteria in the same query to achieve the desired results. Again, using the Northwind Traders database as a basis for an example, you might need a listing of all customers where the Job Title field contains "Owner", located in either Boston or Seattle. To retrieve this data, you would enter **Boston** and **Seattle** in separate criteria rows underneath the City field, and you would enter **Owner** in these same rows underneath the Job Title field. The design of this query is shown in the example on the following page.

Field:	Job Title	Business Phone	Home Phone	Mobile Phone	Fax Number	Address	City
Table:	Customers	Customers	Customers	Customers	Customers	Customers	Customers
Sort:							
Show:	☑	☑			☑	☑	☑
Criteria:	"Owner"						"Boston"
or:	"Owner"						"Seattle"

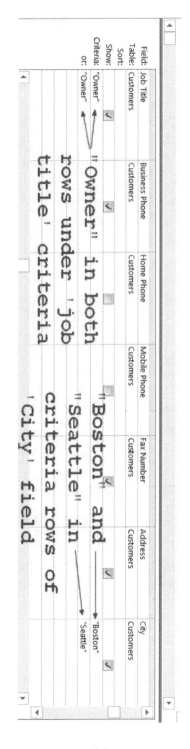

"Owner" in both rows under 'Job title' criteria

"Boston" and "Seattle" in criteria rows of 'City' field

One important point to note in the case of this example is that the expression "owner" has been placed in **both** criteria rows of the query grid. This is required in order to obtain all owners of companies based in Boston and Seattle. If the "owner" criteria were omitted from the second row, the query would interpret this as all owners of companies based in Boston, or all companies based in Seattle.

Available Query Symbols and Operators

When constructing the expressions needed for your criteria entries, you can use any of the symbols and operators shown in Table 3-2. You can combine these symbols within your expressions to select records based on a variety of numeric conditions, ranges, and pattern matches.

Table 3-2 Valid Query Operators

Symbol	Means	Example
=	equals	= Jones
>	greater than	> 8.50
<	less than	< 200
>=	greater than or equal to	>= 6/30/99
<=	less than or equal to	<= 12.50
<>	not equal to	<> Chicago
between	between two values, including the values	between 8 and 19
in	within a set of values	in (USA Mexico Canada)
is null	field contains no data	is null

is not null	field contains data	is not null
like	used for pattern matching	like Mor*
and	both expressions are true	>6/30/11 and <12/31/11
or	either expression is true	USA or CANADA
not	expression is not true	not Mor*
?	pattern matching for any one character	=(202) 555-????
*	pattern matching for any characters	Mor*

The asterisk and question mark symbols are commonly used for "pattern matching", in cases where you need to retrieve records where a text entry in a field matches a given pattern. As the table indicates, the asterisk denotes any number of characters, while the question mark denotes a single character. As an example, for a date field, you might enter the expression:

LIKE * / * / 12

to retrieve records where entries in the date field match any dates in the year 2012. In a text field containing last names, you might use the expression,

LIKE "M*"

to query a last name field for names that might include Morris, Merrick, and Murphy.

In uses of Access that require a "full text search", the asterisk symbol is commonly used to search for text that is contained somewhere within a field. To do this, you include an asterisk both before and after the desired search text. As an example, perhaps you need a listing from a table of documents for a case at a law firm, but you only want to see records where the Summary field (which happens to be a long text field containing large amounts of text) contains the word "mortgage." In the Summary field of the query grid, in the Criteria row, you would enter an expression like ***mortgage*** to retrieve the desired records. You can use this technique with long text fields whenever you need to locate a text string that appears somewhere in the contents of the field.

Querying for Today's Date

You can also query a date field for records matching the current date (according to the computer's system clock). To do this, use the date function in Access, which is DATE(). As an example, if you were to enter the following expression:

date( )

in the criteria cell for a date field, the query would retrieve records where the entry in that field matches the current date. You can also query a date field for records that match a calculation based on the current date. You could use an expression like the following in a query containing a date field:

between #6/15/11# and date( )

to retrieve all records with a date falling between June 15, 2011 and the current date. You could retrieve all records falling within the past 90 days with an expression like

between date( ) and date( ) - 90

Entering Expressions

Access is very flexible in the manner in which it will accept expressions. You can enter text with or without quotes, and you can precede the text with an equal symbol, or omit the equal symbol. (When you move out of the criteria cell or when the query runs, Access inserts quotes around any text strings.) Hence, all of the following expressions would have the same result if used in a text field of a query:

Chicago

"Chicago"

=Chicago

You can enter dates using all commonly-accepted date formats. The # symbol surrounding dates is optional, but Access automatically will add the symbol around a date value that you enter into a query. As an example of dates, any of the following entries could be used in a query:

Apr 30 12

#4/30/12#

30 April 2012

4/30/12

30-Apr-12

You can enter logical (yes/no) values as Yes or No, True or False, On or Off, or as numeric values of -1 (meaning yes) and 0 (meaning no).

Using the Is Null Operator

Access offers a special operator, **Is Null**, which can be used whenever you need to retrieve a set of records where there is no data in a field. (Note that this is *not* the same as simply leaving a field in the query grid empty. An empty field in the query grid tells Access that it does not matter what is in that field in a given record.) The term **Is Null** indicates that the field must be empty before the record will appear in the resulting dynaset. Access also offers an opposite expression, **Is Not Null**, that can be used to indicate that the field must contain some kind of data.

Using the NOT Operator

In some cases, you may need to query a table for records that do not match a particular value. As an example, you might want to see all customers who do not live in Philadelphia. You can do this with the use of the NOT operator within the query expression. For example, in a City field, you might enter the expression **Not "Philadelphia"** to find all records from cities other than Philadelphia.

Using Ranges

Table 3-2 also contains examples of the use of *range operators*, which are commonly used to retrieve all records that fall within a certain range. Range operators are commonly used with date/time and with number fields, but they can be used with text, as well. You could design a query to retrieve all records with last names from the letters A through M, or you could use a date field in a table to retrieve all records containing a date entry that falls between the first day and the last day of a certain month. As an example, entering the following expression

Between "M" and "Zz"

in the Last name criteria column of a query grid would result in the retrieval of all last names beginning with the letters M through Z. In this example, note the inclusion of the second letter *z*. It is necessary, because if it were omitted, Access would retrieve all names up to Z, but none following the letter Z alone. (The resulting dynaset would omit all last names containing more than one character and beginning with the letter Z.) Another example of a criteria involving ranges would be with a date field, with a criteria entry like the one shown here:

between 6/1/11 and 12/31/11

In this case, the query would include all records with dates in the field that fall between June 15, 2011 and December 31, 2011.

Omitting Fields from the Results

If you need a certain field in a query's design in order to use criteria, but you want to omit that field from appearing in the resulting dynaset, you can easily do so. To omit any field from the results of a query, click the Show check box for that field to remove the X in the box. (By default, an X appears in the Show check box for any field included in the query, indicating that the field will be included in the results.) Note that you cannot omit any fields that you plan to use in forms or reports that are based on the query.

Adding Calculated Fields to Queries

In addition to actual fields that exist in the underlying table, you can also include *calculated fields* in the design of a query. Calculated fields do not exist in any table. Instead, they contain calculations that result from an expression. (The expression is usually based on number or date/time fields in the underlying table.) To create a calculated field in a query's design, enter the expression that will perform the calculation in an empty cell in the Field row. You can precede the expression with a name and a colon; if you do this, that name will be used for the field name in the query's dynaset. If you omit a name and colon, the field in the resulting dynaset will be labeled ExprN, where N is a numeric value starting with 1 for the first calculated field used, and increasing by 1 for each additional calculated field in the query.

As an example, if a query based on a table in a Billing database contained fields for Hourly Rate and Hours, you could create a calculated field named Total Amount by entering an expression like this one in an empty cell of the Field row:

Total Amount: [Hourly Rate]*[Hours]

And when the query runs, Access would multiply each of the values in the Hourly Rate field by the corresponding values in the Hours field to produce the new values, which would be stored in the field named Total Amount. Table 3-3 shows examples of expressions that you might use to create calculated fields within a query:

Table 3-3

expression	*results*
[Salary] * 1.06	The salary plus 6%
New Salary:[Salary] * 1.1	The salary plus 10%, to appear in a column labeled 'New Salary'
Limit Date:[Date Stored] + 90	A date 90 days after the value stored in the 'Date Stored' field, to appear in a column labeled 'Limit Date'
Name:[First Name] & " " & [Last Name]	The values in the First Name and Last Name fields, separated by a space and placed in a column to be labeled 'Name'

Another common use for calculated fields in queries is to *concatenate*, or combine, text strings. To do this, include the concatenation operator (&) as a part of the expression. As an example, you could create a calculated field in a query that would combine the Last Name, First Name, and Middle Initial fields into a single name using an expression like the following:

[First Name] & " " & [Middle Initial] & ". " & [Last Name]

Saving Queries

To use your queries at a later time (or as data sources for your forms or reports), you will need to save them. To save a query, click the Save icon at the upper-left corner of the window. If you are saving a query for the first time, a dialog box appears asking for a name for the new query. Enter a desired name (up to 64 characters in length, and spaces are allowed), then click OK.

Alternately, you can also press Ctrl+F4 to save a query. If you have made any changes since opening the Query window, you will be asked if you want to save the changes. Click Yes in the dialog box, and the query will be saved.

Printing Queries

You can print the contents of queries, in much the same manner as you can print tables. Doing so can provide you with a "quick-and-dirty" report containing the data you need, although a report created in this manner will not contain the precise formatting offered by reports that you design in Access. You can print a query using these steps:

1. Run the query, to show the resulting dynaset.

2. If you desire only certain records within the query, select those records by clicking and dragging along the record selectors at the left edge of the query window.

3.   Click the File tab in the ribbon, and choose Print.

4.   When the Print dialog box appears, if you selected certain records, click the Selection button in the dialog box. Choose any other desired options in the dialog box, then click OK.

> **TIP:** You can obtain a fast, formatted report of your query data by using the Report Wizard to create a report based on the query. Create a new report using the Report Wizard (see Chapter 5 for additional details). In the Select A Table/Query list box that appears within the New Report dialog box, choose your query by name as the source of the records, then answer the remaining questions asked by the Report Wizard and save the report.

A Hands-On Example of Query Creation

As a hands-on example, perhaps you need a listing of all sales contacts located in a particular city, such as Hayward, CA. **The hands-on example will be used by forms and reports in the remainder of this book, so you may wish to take the time to learn the use of queries by following the steps in the hands-on exercises below.** Perform the following steps:

Open the Access database you created in Chapter 2, if it is not already open.

In the ribbon area, click the Create tab.

In the Queries portion of the ribbon, click Query Design. A new query appears in the lower portion of the window, and the Show Table dialog box appears above the window (see illustration).

Select the Sales Contacts table in the list box, click Add, and then click Close.

In the Sales Contacts list box, click on the Last name field and drag it to the first empty column of the field row in the query. Click on the First name field and drag it to the next empty column of the field row in the query. Click on the Company field and drag it to the next empty column of the field row in the query.

Scroll down in the list box, click on the City field and drag it to the next empty column of the field row in the query. Finally, click on the Phone field and drag it to the next empty column of the field row in the query.

Click in the Criteria row under the City column, and enter Hayward.

At this point, your query should resemble the following. You've completed your first query, and you can now run the query to observe the results.

Click the Run button in the Ribbon area (it's the button containing the large red exclamation point). Assuming you are using the sample data typed while following the directions outlined earlier, the results will resemble the illustration that follows.

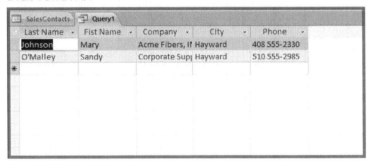

*Open the File menu and choose Save, to save the completed query. Access will display a dialog box asking for a name for the query; for this example, type **Hayward customers** and click OK.*

Once the query has been saved, it appears as a separate object in the Navigation pane at the far left, as shown in the following illustration.

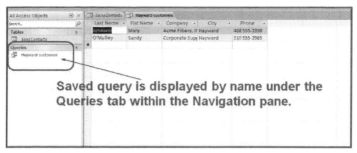

Saved query is displayed by name under the Queries tab within the Navigation pane.

For another hands-on example, consider a need to see all customers in one state (California), and in this example, you want to see the data sorted `alphabetically by name. Perform these steps:

In the ribbon area, click the Create tab.

Click Query Design. A new query appears in the lower portion of the window, and the Show Table dialog box again appears above the window.

Select the Sales Contacts table in the list box, click Add, then click Close.

For this example, you will add all the fields to the grid with one step. Double-click the table name 'Sale Contacts' at the top of the Fields List. When you do so, all the fields will appear selected as a group.

Click and drag any field in the list to any blank area of the first column in the grid. When you do this, the fields will be added to the window as a group (see illustration).

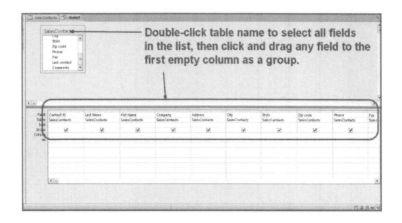

Double-click table name to select all fields in the list, then click and drag any field to the first empty column as a group.

To set the sort order, click at the intersection of the Sort row and the Last name column, and change the drop-down that appears to 'Ascending.' Then move to the right by one column, and repeat this step for the 'First name' column.

Click in the Criteria row under the City column, and enter **CA** then click the Run button in the toolbar (the one with the large red exclamation point) to run the query. Assuming you are using the sample data typed while following the directions outlined earlier, the results will resemble the illustration that follows.

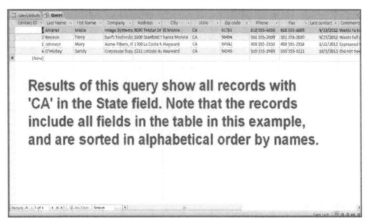

Results of this query show all records with 'CA' in the State field. Note that the records include all fields in the table in this example, and are sorted in alphabetical order by names.

108

*Open the File menu and choose Save. When asked for a name for the query, enter **All fields California only** and click OK.*

Using Queries to Draw Relationships

As the previous chapter mentioned, you can draw relationships between tables using either of two methods. One way (described in Chapter 2) is to use the Database Tools/Relationships option to create the relationships at the table level. The other approach involves creating a relational query. A relational query is similar in overall design to a non-relational query; the only significant difference is that you add more than one table to the query, and you establish a link between the tables (by dragging a field in one Field List to a related field in another Field List). Here are the steps you can use to create a relational query:

1.   Click the Create tab, then click Query Design. This causes a new query window to appear, with the Show Table dialog box above it.

2.   In the Show Table dialog box, add each table needed by the relational query to the query design by selecting each table and clicking Add (or by double-clicking the table).

3.   Create the relational link needed between the tables by dragging the common field from one Field List to another. As you do this, join lines appear between the common fields in the tables. (If you previously established relationships at the database level using the Edit/Relationships command, Access will add the join lines automatically.)

4.   Add the necessary fields to the query, using the same techniques you would use to design any query.

5.   Add any needed sorting and selection criteria to the query's design.

6. Save and run the query.

As an example, here is a relational query based on three tables, with join lines established between the Product ID field of the Order Details table, and the matching ID fields of the Products and Suppliers tables. Fields have been added to the query from all three tables.

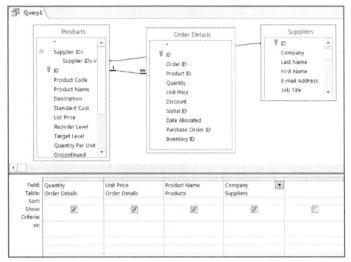

The design of a query based on multiple tables

The following figure shows the results when the query is run.

Order Details ▾	Order Details ▾	Products.Product Name ▾	Suppliers.Cor ▾
100	$14.00	Northwind Traders Beer	Supplier D
30	$3.50	Northwind Traders Dried Plums	Supplier B
10	$30.00	Northwind Traders Dried Pears	Supplier B
10	$53.00	Northwind Traders Dried Apples	Supplier B
10	$3.50	Northwind Traders Dried Plums	Supplier B
15	$18.00	Northwind Traders Chai	Supplier D
20	$46.00	Northwind Traders Coffee	Supplier C
20	$46.00	Northwind Traders Coffee	Supplier D
30	$9.20	Northwind Traders Chocolate Biscuits Mix	Supplier A
20	$9.20	Northwind Traders Chocolate Biscuits Mix	Supplier A
10	$12.75	Northwind Traders Chocolate	Supplier J
200	$9.65	Northwind Traders Clam Chowder	Supplier F
17	$40.00	Northwind Traders Curry Sauce	Supplier H
300	$46.00	Northwind Traders Coffee	Supplier C
300	$46.00	Northwind Traders Coffee	Supplier D
100	$12.75	Northwind Traders Chocolate	Supplier J
200	$2.99	Northwind Traders Green Tea	Supplier C
300	$46.00	Northwind Traders Coffee	Supplier C
300	$46.00	Northwind Traders Coffee	Supplier D
10	$25.00	Northwind Traders Boysenberry Spread	Supplier B
10	$25.00	Northwind Traders Boysenberry Spread	Supplier F
10	$22.00	Northwind Traders Cajun Seasoning	Supplier J
10	$9.20	Northwind Traders Chocolate Biscuits Mix	Supplier A

Record: 1 of 67   No Filter   Search

The results of a query based on multiple tables

If Access adds a join line that you don't want, you can easily delete it. To delete the unwanted line, click it to select it, then press the Del key. If you want to remove a table that you've added to a query's design, just click anywhere within the Field List for the table and press the Del key.

Notes about Relational Queries

There are certain limitations to the data produced by relational queries, and you should be aware of these limitations. Data in relational queries based on one-to-one relationships can be edited as long as there are no totals or crosstabs, and as long as the Unique Values Only query property is not turned on. If a relational query is based on a one-to-many relationship, you can only edit records on the "many" side of the relationship. If the query includes more than two tables, only the table at the end of the "many" side can be edited.

111

A warning about missing joins

If you omit a join line in an Access table, the resulting dynaset is incorrect and displays a ridiculously large amount of data. The reason is that when a join line is left out of a query, Access joins every record in one table with every record in the other table. The result is something called a *Cartesian product*, or a cross product of the two tables. For example, omitting a join for a query containing two tables (each having 200 records) produces a dynaset with 40,000 records, of which 39,800 of the records are absolutely meaningless.

Using Parameter Queries

If you routinely run the same query repeatedly, entering a different criteria in a certain criteria cell each time you run the query, you can save time by creating a *parameter query*. A parameter query is a select query that asks for a parameter each time the query runs. You can use the existing queries in your database as the basis for parameter queries. Instead of having to open the query in Design view and entering the new criteria into the query grid each time, Access will display dialog boxes with prompts, asking you for the criteria. You can create a parameter query with the following steps:

1.   Design a select query, using the techniques outlined earlier in this chapter.

2.   In the Criteria cells directly beneath the fields that you want to use as parameters, enter your parameter text, enclosed in square brackets. (This text will appear as a prompt in the dialog box that Access displays when the query runs.) For example, if you wanted a parameter in a Order Date field to ask for a desired date when the query runs, you could enter an expression like **[Enter the date of the order:]** in the Order Date field. Be

careful to use text that is different then your field names. The figure that follows shows parameter text entered in the Order Date field of a query.

3. Save the query by choosing File/Save from the menus, or pressing Ctrl+F4 and answering Yes to the prompt that appears.

4. When you run the query, a dialog box like the one shown after the query's design illustration appears, asking for the parameter value. When you enter the data and click OK, the query runs and provides the data according to your criteria.

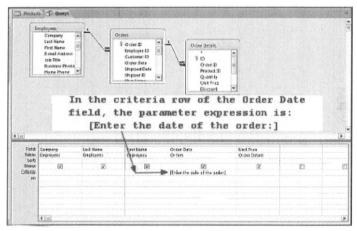

The parameter text entered into Order Date field of a table

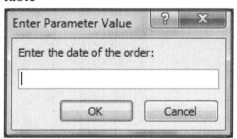

The dialog box produced by the above parameter query

While the example described above used a parameter with a single value, you are not limited to a single value in a parameter. One common use of multiple values in the same parameter is to prompt for a range of acceptable values. This design technique is often used with numbers, currency amounts, or dates. For example, consider a query based on a table that contains a date field for the start date for a group of seasonal employees. If you want a parameter query that prompts for all employees who started at the company between two dates, you could enter:

between [Enter the starting date:] and [Enter the ending date:]

in the criteria cell for the date field. When you run the query, Access first would ask for the starting date, then for the ending date. The resulting records shown in the query would contain only those records falling between the two dates.

TIP: Parameter queries are excellent data sources for reports that require different sets of data each time the report runs. As an example, if your database has a billing report and that report needs to be produced on a monthly basis, you can base the report on a parameter query that asks for the starting date and the ending date of invoices. That way each time the report runs, you enter the appropriate dates for that month, and the resulting report contains records from the desired month's invoices.

Using Action Queries

While you can use select queries to retrieve specific data for editing or for inclusion in forms and reports, action queries perform a specified action on the data retrieved by the query. You can use action queries to copy records into new tables, to add records from one table to another, to update values in certain fields, or to delete groups of records. In Access, you can create

114

four types of action queries: *make table queries*, which create new tables; *update queries*, which change data in existing tables; *append queries*, which copy records from one table to another; and *delete queries*, which delete a group of records from a table.

The process of designing action queries starts out in the same manner as the process of designing select queries; you design a query that retrieves the data you want to perform an action upon. Then, you convert the select query into an action query by choosing the appropriate query type from the Query menu while in Design view.

Creating Append Queries

When you need to add records from one table to another table, you can use append queries. The records are copied from the original (source) table to the destination table, so the records will remain in the original table after the append query has been run. (If you want to remove the records from the original table, you can use a delete query to do so.) You can create an append query using the following steps.

1.   Design and test a select query that retrieves the records you want to append to the other table.

2.   While in Design view for the query, click the Append button in the ribbon to change the query into an Append query. When you do this, the Append dialog box appears, as shown in the figure that follows.

3.   In the Table Name box, type the name of the table the records should be appended to, or click the down arrow and choose an existing table name from the list. (To append the records to a table stored in a different database, click the Another Database button in the dialog box, then enter the name of the database in the File Name text box.)

Then click OK. Access will add an Append To row to the query grid.

4.   Enter the field names from the table you are appending records to in the Append To row, matching them to the existing fields in the Field row. (Where the field names are the same, Access automatically displays the field names in the Append To row.) *Note:* The Append To row and the Field row of your append queries must contain the same number of fields.

5.   Run the query by clicking the Run button in the ribbon. Access displays a confirmation dialog, telling you how many records will be added to the table. Click OK to run the query and append the records.

The Append dialog box for an append query

If you use an append query to add data to another table and that table has an AutoNumber field, you can keep the value in the AutoNumber field from the original table, or you can cause Access to use new values in the AutoNumber field. To keep the AutoNumber values from the original table, include the AutoNumber field in the query grid when designing the append query. To cause Access to add new AutoNumber values, omit the AutoNumber field from the design of the append query.

116

Creating Delete Queries

When you want to delete a group of records as a single operation, you do so by means of a delete query. A delete query is simply a select query that deletes all the records retrieved by the query. You can use the following steps to create a delete query.

1. Design and test a select query that retrieves the records you want deleted from the table.

2. While still in Design view, click the Delete button in the ribbon. A "Delete Where" row will be added to the query grid, indicating that the query, when run, will delete the records.

3. Run the query by clicking the Run button on the ribbon. A confirmation dialog box appears, telling you how many records will be deleted from the table.

4. Click OK to run the query and delete the records.

Note that the effects of a delete query *cannot* be undone. You should be sure that you want to perform the deletion before running a delete query.

Creating Update Queries

Update queries are action queries that update (or make a specific change to) all records that meet a certain criteria. Update queries are commonly used whenever you need to change a large amount of data in a global fashion. As an example, you might need to give a new telephone area code to all customers based in a particular city; rather than manually editing each customer record, you could structure an update query to perform the task. As with other action queries, you first design a select query that retrieves the records that you want to update. Then while still in Design view, you choose Query/Update from the menus or click the Update Query button on the ribbon to change the type of query from a select query into an update query. Access adds an Update To row to the query, and you place criteria in this row that tells Access how you want to update the data. Use the following steps to create an update query.

1. Design and test a select query that retrieves the records that you want to update.

2. While still in Design view, click the Update button in the ribbon. An Update To row appears within the query grid.

3. In the Update To cell for the field that you want to update, enter a desired expression or a value that will change the data. As an example, you could increase rates by $10.00 in an Hourly Rate field by entering **[Hourly Rate] + 10**. If you wanted to change all area codes for residents of Rocky Mount, North Carolina from 919 to 252, you would enter **Rocky Mount** in the criteria cell of the City field, **NC** in the criteria cell of the State field, and **252** in the Update To cell for the Area Code field.

4. Run the query by clicking the Run button on the ribbon. A confirmation dialog box appears, telling you how many records will be updated. Click OK to run the query and update the records.

Creating Make-Table Queries

You can use make-table queries to create new tables based on existing records in another table. The records retrieved by the query are copied into the new table (the original records remain intact in the original table). Make-table queries are commonly used for exporting selected data to other file formats, and for backing up or "archiving" important information. You can create a make-table query using the following steps:

1.   Design and test a select query that retrieves the records you want to insert into the new table.

2.   While still in Design view, click the Make Table button in the ribbon. The Make Table dialog box appears, as shown in the following figure.

3.   In the Table Name box, type the name for the new table, or click the down arrow and choose a table name from the list if you want to overwrite an existing table with the results of the make table query. (Optionally, you can create the new table in a different database. To do this, click the Another Database button in the dialog box and enter the name of the database in the File Name text box.) When you have completed the options in the dialog box, click OK.

4.   Run the query by clicking the Run button on the ribbon. A confirmation dialog box appears, telling you how many records will be added to the new table. Click OK to run the query and create the new table.

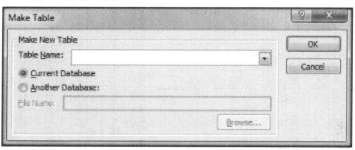

The Make Table dialog box

Note: When you create a new table by using a make-table query, Access does not transfer any key field specifications, nor does it transfer any field properties to the new table. If you had specific field properties or key fields designated in the original table, you may want to open the new table in Design view, and set the same properties or key fields.

A note about SQL and your queries

If you are familiar with the database language SQL (structured query language), you may want to know that Access uses SQL as the underlying language behind queries. Although the query is usually designed visually while working in the design view window, when you save the query, Access translates the visual design into a SQL statement which it processes when you run the query. You can view the SQL statement used by any query by opening the query in design view, then choosing SQL View from the File menu. A query's design window then displays the underlying SQL statement for the query, such as the one shown here.

Although you can directly edit the language used in the SQL statement, Microsoft doesn't recommend doing this unless you are intimately familiar with the SQL syntax used by Access. However, advanced users may find it worthwhile knowing how SQL works behind the scenes in Access, because you can use SQL statements directly inside of the record source properties of your forms and reports.

Summary

This chapter has provided a wealth of information about queries, an important feature of Access. You learned how to design select queries to retrieve the data you need for editing, for forms and reports; how to design relational queries to draw data from multiple tables; and how to create action queries to perform various tasks. In the next chapter, you will learn how to create and use forms, to view and edit your data in Access.

Chapter 4 - Creating and Using Access Forms

The previous chapters demonstrated how you can enter data directly into Access tables by typing the data directly into a datasheet (or into a query's dynaset). And this can be an easy and straightforward way to enter data. However, such a "direct" means of data entry has its disadvantages, as well. You (or anyone else) must be familiar with Access to enter data directly into tables or queries; field names may be cryptic in appearance to office novices; and few safeguards exist against incorrect data entry. And, if the table contains a large number of fields, it is difficult or impossible to see all of the fields without repeated scrolling of the datasheet window.

To get around these limitations, you can use *forms* for your data entry and editing. With forms, you have full control over precisely where the fields appear as you design the form. And you can build rules into forms that prevent others from entering incorrect data. In addition to data entry and editing, you can also use forms for printing data (although this is more typically done using reports, as discussed in the next chapter). In this chapter, you'll learn to design and use forms to add data, and to view and edit the data stored in your tables. A typical form is shown here.

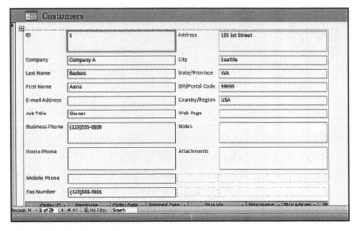

A typical form in Access

Access provides a number of ways to create forms. If your form is based on a single table or query, you can create a default form in a matter of seconds, using the Form option on the Create tab of the ribbon. You can also use a feature known as the Form Wizards to quickly create a variety of forms based on a single table, or on multiple tables. And if you prefer to maintain full control over the form creation process, you can design your own forms manually. Often, you can save time when designing forms by combining the last two methods; you can use the Form Wizards to initially create the form, then make additional changes to the form manually.

Creating a Form with the Form Option

If you want to create a form that is based on a single table or query, the simplest way to do this is to use the Form option found on the Create tab. The Form option creates a simple single-column form for whatever table or query is selected in the navigation pane when you click the button. To create a form using the Form option, perform these steps:

124

1. Select the desired table or query to be used as a source of data for the form in the navigation pane.

2. Click the Create tab in the ribbon area, then click the Form icon. In a moment, Access builds a default form for the table or query; an example of such a form was shown earlier, at the start of this chapter.

When you use the Form feature to create a form, you get a form like the one shown at the start of this chapter. As many of the fields as will fit are aligned at the left side of the form (the remainder may appear in a second column on the right), and the field names are used as the default labels for the fields. If you want to change any of these design aspects of the form, you can easily do so by opening the form in Design view, and making changes to the form manually, as detailed later in this chapter.

Creating a Form with the Form Wizards

When you want a little more control over the end result (or when you need to create a form based on two tables) but you still want Access to help you with the overall process, you can use the Form Wizards to assist you in the creation of your forms. Like all wizards in Access, the Form Wizards ask you a series of questions and produce a finished, ready-to-use object (in this case, a form) based on your answers to the questions. What follows are the overall steps you'll use to create forms with the Form Wizards. The paragraphs that follow these steps describe the steps in greater detail.

1. In the ribbon area, click the Create tab.

2. Within the Forms area of the tab, click Form Wizard.

3. Follow the directions and answer the appropriate questions that appear in the wizard

dialog boxes. In the last dialog box that appears, click 'Open the form with data in it' then click Finish to begin entering or viewing data in Form view, or click 'Modify the form's design' then click Finish to open the form in Design view, where you can make additional changes to the design of the form.

That's the process of using the Form Wizards, in a nutshell. Now, here is the process in greater detail:

When you click the Create tab in the ribbon and then click Form Wizard, the first dialog box for the Form Wizards appears, as shown in the figure that follows.

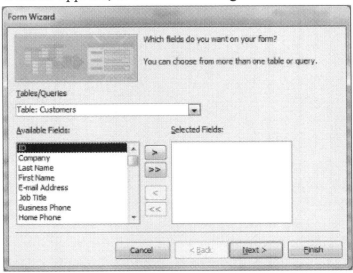

Initial dialog box of the Form Wizards

Choosing the Tables and the Desired Fields

At the top of the dialog box is a Tables/Queries list box. As you select a desired table or query from this list, the fields in that table or query appear below, in the Available Fields portion of the dialog box. You can click on any field to select it, then click the Right Arrow button to add the field to the Selected Fields list at the right side of the dialog box. (Alternately, you can double-click any field in the Available Fields list box, to add it to the Selected Fields list box.) If you want to include all the fields in the table or query in the form, just click the double right-arrow button. If you make a mistake and add a field you don't want in the form, select it in the Selected Fields list box, then click the left arrow button to remove that field from the list.

If you want to create a *relational form* (a form that is based on more than one table or query), first add all the desired fields from the first table (or query). Then choose another table (or query) in the Tables/Queries list box, and add the desired fields for that table or query. Once you have finished adding all the fields needed by your form, click Next.

The dialog box that appears next depends on whether you have chosen fields from a single table or query, or from more than one table or query. If the chosen fields are from a single table or query, you will see the dialog box shown in the figure that follows.

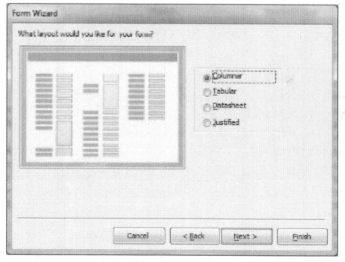

Second Form Wizard dialog box (used for single tables)

127

Here you are asked to choose a layout for the form (your choices are Columnar, Tabular, or Datasheet). If you select Columnar, the fields are arranged in a single column, at the left side of the form. The Tabular option creates a form with an appearance that resembles a table's datasheet, but with blank space surrounding each field. The Datasheet option results in a form with an appearance virtually identical to that of a datasheet. Choose the desired layout in the dialog box, then click Next.

If you are using the Form Wizard to create a form based on multiple tables and/or queries, the next dialog box that you see is the one shown in the figure that follows.

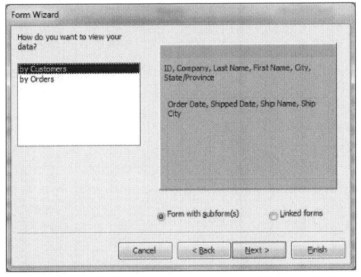

Second Form Wizard dialog box (used for multiple tables)

The left side of this dialog box asks you how you want to view the data, and it provides a list of the tables or queries you have chosen earlier to provide the data to the form. In effect, you are deciding which table (or query) should be the *parent table*, or the table with the highest priority. (To make a selection, you click the desired table in the list at the left side of

128

the dialog box.) Once you choose the parent table, you can also use the options at the bottom of the dialog box to choose Form with Subforms (if you want the data shown on a single form), or Linked Forms (if you want the data shown on multiple forms). If you select Form with Subforms (the default), Access creates a form that displays one record at a time from the parent table, and all associated records from the linked or "child" table. If you select Linked Forms, Access creates two or more forms, and the additional forms are linked to the first form. When done with the options in this dialog box, click Next.

If you are using the Form Wizard to design a form based on multiple tables and you chose Form with Subforms as the previous option, you will now see a dialog box like the example shown below. This dialog box asks whether you want the subform (the related 'child' records) displayed as a tabular format, or as a datasheet. Make your desired selection and click Next.

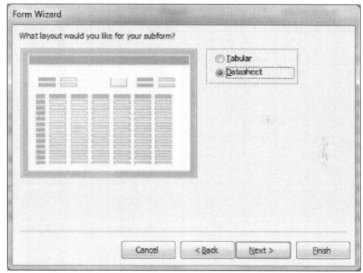

Third Form Wizard dialog box (used for multiple tables)

Completing the Design Process

The last dialog box that appears (see the figure that follows) asks for a title for the form. If the form is based on more than one table or query, you will also be asked for a title for any subforms that have been created during the process. A default title is provided (which is the same as the primary table or query that the form was based upon), and you can leave this title, or change it to any title you wish. Additionally, the options in the dialog box let you open the form to view or enter information, or open the form in 'Design view' where you can make further modifications to the design of the form. Once you click Finish, the Form Wizard completes the process of creating the form.

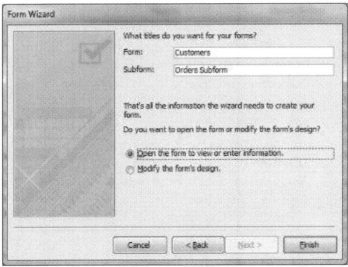

Last dialog box for Form Wizards

Once the form has been saved, it appears in the Navigation pane under the Forms section, and you can double-click the form by name to open the form in Form view, where you can add and edit data. For more details on working with the form, see "Saving and Using the Form" later in this chapter.

Designing Forms Manually? Let the Form Wizards Lend a Hand!

In some cases you may prefer to design your own forms. However, you shouldn't ignore the helpful capabilities of the Form Wizards. You can usually save considerable time and effort by letting the Form Wizards create a form, then you can open that form in Design view, and modify the form as desired (using the techniques described in the next section of this chapter).

Designing Forms Manually

If you prefer the "roll-your-own" method of forms creation, you can design your own forms from scratch, using the manual method of form design. You open a blank form, size the form to the desired width and height, and add the desired *design objects* such as text boxes that display the contents of fields, labels, and graphics, to the form. The overall steps behind the manual method of forms creation are as follows:

1. In the ribbon area, click the Create tab.

2. In the Forms area of the ribbon, click the Form Design button to open a new, empty form in the main portion of the window. (An example is shown in the illustration that follows.)

3. Open the Property Sheet for the form, click the Data tab, and choose the table or query that should serve as the primary source of data for the form.

4. Using the Form Design Tools that appear in the ribbon area along with the 'Add Existing Fields' icon in the ribbon, place the desired objects (text boxes, labels, and any other types of controls that are needed) on the form.

5. Click the Save icon at the upper left to save the completed form.

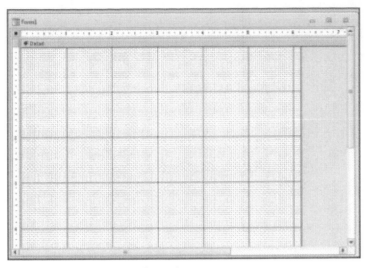

A blank form in Design view

In addition to manually creating forms from scratch, you can also open existing forms that have been created with the Form option or with the Form Wizards in Design view. To do so, right-click the form's name in the Navigation pane, and choose Design View from the menu that appears. The following figure shows an example of an existing form, created using the Form Wizards, that has been opened in Design View.

An existing form open in Design view

Existing forms will usually contain *text box controls*, which are used to display the data contained in the fields of the table or query. Forms also typically contain *label controls*, which provide the user with feedback about the various objects on the form, or about how to use the form. Optionally, forms can contain form headers and form footers. Also, some forms may contain *command buttons*; these let you add greater functionality to a form.

The Design Surface

When you create a form manually, it initially opens to a default size, as shown in the previous illustration. Rulers appear at the top and left edges of the form, and a grid composed of dots fills the drawing area by default. You can change the size of the form as necessary, to accommodate as many fields or other objects as you may need. Use the following steps to change the size of a form:

    1. While in Design view, place the pointer on the bottom edge or right edge of the form. The pointer changes to a double-headed arrow.

2. Drag the pointer up or down to change the height of the form, or drag the pointer left or right to change the width of the form.

Adding Controls to Forms

As you design forms, most objects you add to the form (such as labels, and text boxes that display fields) are called *controls*. If you are going to do much work with forms in Design view, you must know how to add controls, move them, and size them as needed. You will find these skills to be useful when designing reports, because many of the same techniques used in form design are also used when manually designing reports. In Access, you can add three types of controls to forms (or to reports). They are *bound controls, unbound controls,* and *calculated controls.*

- **Bound controls-** These are controls that are connected to a field of the table or query that the form is based upon. In the figure shown previously, the text boxes that display the contents of the fields are bound controls. The most commonly-used type of bound control is the text box control. However, other types of bound controls can be used in forms (and reports), such as check boxes, list boxes, toggle buttons, and object frames (which typically display photos stored in OLE fields of a table).

- **Unbound controls-** These are controls that are not connected to any fields of a table or query. In forms created by the Form Wizards, the title that appears in the form header and the labels containing the names of the fields are unbound controls.

- **Calculated controls-** These are controls that display the results of a calculation. The expression used to perform the calculation is typically based on one or more fields of a table.

You add controls to forms using the variety of tools that appear in the ribbon area when you have a form open in Design View. These tools are shown in the figure.on the following page.

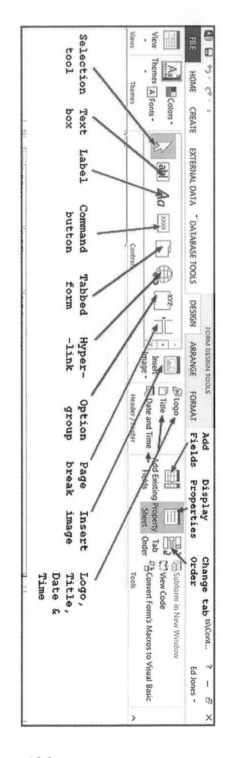

When you want to add bound controls to a form, the easiest way to do so is to use the Field List. Click the Add Existing Fields button at the right side of the ribbon, and choose the table or query from the list that appears at the right. Once you select a table or query, a list of fields from that table or query will be displayed.

Assuming the type of control you want to create is a text box, you just drag the desired field from the Field List to the desired location on the form. When you release the mouse button, a text box bound to the appropriate field appears.

You can add multiple fields to the form as text boxes in a single operation, by selecting the first field in the Field List, then holding the Ctrl key as you select each additional desired field in the list. Once all the needed fields are highlighted, click on any selected field, and drag the fields onto the form as a group. (Note that if the fields are too close together for your liking, you can easily space them apart by clicking the 'Arrange' tab under 'Form Design Tools' in the ribbon, and then using the various options shown under 'Size/Space' in the ribbon.)

To add other types of controls to a form, you use the assortment of tools shown in the previous illustration. The various tools and their uses are described in the list that follows.

- *Selection tool - Selects, moves, or sizes objects within the form. If another tool was previously selected, clicking the Selection tool deselects that tool.*

- *Text Box - Used to create a text box that displays the contents of a field, or the results of an expression. Text boxes are usually bound (or tied) to a field in a table or a query.*

- *Label - Used to add a label, commonly used as descriptive text, titles, captions, or instructions.*

- *Command Button - Used to add a command button. Command buttons are typically attached to macros or to Visual Basic for Applications program code. By default, adding a command button causes a wizard to appear that assists in the creation of the desired type of command button.*

- *Tabbed Form - Used to add a tabbed form control to a form's design. You can then place other controls on each of the tabs.*

- *Hyperlink - Used to add a reference to a hyperlink to a form.*

- *Option Group - Used to add option groups. Option groups are used to store two or more option buttons, toggle buttons, or check boxes; only one of the options in an option group can be selected at a time.*

- *Option Button - Used to add an option button. Option buttons are circles that appear darkened in the center when selected. Option buttons (also called radio buttons) can be used in an option group to choose a single choice from many, or they can be used individually to specify a yes/no choice.*

- *Page Break - Used to insert a page break into the form. (Page breaks force the start of a new page when a form is printed, but they are not visible when the form is viewed.)*

- *Combo Box - Used to create a combination box. Combination boxes act as a combination of a list box and a text box. Using a combination box, you can choose values from a pull-down list within the box, or you can type in a value. The choices in the list are generally taken from rows of a query, but they can also be based on a list of predetermined values.*

- *Chart - Used to add a chart to a form. This tool launches a chart wizard, which you use to design a chart based on values in the table or query that supplies data to the form.*

- *Line - Used to draw lines in a form. (Lines are typically used in forms to provide a visual separation of other objects.)*

- *Toggle Button - Used to add a toggle button. Toggle buttons are buttons that appear to have been pushed down when selected. They can be used individually to specify a yes/no choice, or they can be used in option groups to select a single choice from many.*

- *List Box - Used to create a list box. List boxes are used to display values from a predetermined list. The choices in the list are often based on rows of a query, but they can also be based on a list of predetermined values.*

- *Rectangle - Used to add rectangles or squares to a form.*

- *Check Box - Used to add a check box. Check boxes are small squares that contain an 'X' when selected. Check boxes can be used in an option group to choose a single choice from many, or they can be used individually to specify a yes/no choice.*

- *Insert Image - Used to add a frame used to display a static (unchanging) graphic image.*

To create a label, click the Label tool. On the form, click where you want to place the label, type the text for the label, and press Enter. (You can change the label's font and size, if desired, by selecting it and then choosing the desired font and font size from the font options shown in the ribbon.)

The exact steps for creating other types of controls will depend on the type of control, but here are the overall steps you can use:

1.   If the form tools are not already visible in the ribbon, click the Design tab to display them.

2.   Click the tool representing the desired type of control you want to create.

3.   Click in the form where you want to place the upper-left corner of the control, and drag the pointer to size the control to the desired size. If a wizard is appropriate to the type of control you are adding, you can follow the directions in the Control Wizard dialog boxes that appear.

Moving, Sizing, and Deleting Controls

As you work with controls, you will often want to move them, or change the size of controls. To move a control, first select the control by clicking anywhere within the control. Then move the pointer to any edge of the control where the pointer changes shape to a double arrow, and drag the control to the desired location.

> **TIP:** You can move a group of controls in one operation, by first selecting the controls as a group. To do this, select the first control, then hold the Shift key as you select each additional desired control. When all the controls are selected, you can move the pointer to any edge of any selected control where the pointer

> changes shape to a double arrow, and drag the
> controls as a group to the desired location.

To resize a control, select the control by clicking on it. Then move the pointer to any of the control's sizing handles (where the pointer changes shape to a double arrow), and click and drag the control to the desired size.

To move a text box control separately from its label, place the pointer over the handle at the upper-left corner of the text box, where the pointer changes to a hand with a pointing finger. Then click and drag the text box to the desired location.

To delete a control that is not wanted, select the control, then press the Del key.

> **TIP:** Occasionally, you will want to move controls
> very small distances. You can easily do this by
> selecting the control, then holding the Ctrl key
> depressed and using the arrow keys.

Changing a Control's Properties

Controls have *properties* that affect how the control behaves when the form is used, and you can put these properties to use in designing your forms for ease of use and accurate data entry. To change the properties of a control, first select the control by clicking on it. Then click the Property Sheet button in the ribbon. When you do this, a Property sheet appears at the right for the selected control. The following figure shows the Property sheet for a text box control, the type of control most commonly used in forms.

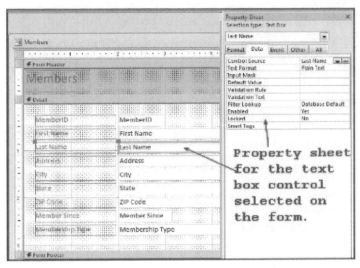

Property sheet for the text box control selected on the form.

The Property sheet for a text box control

Notice that the Property Sheet groups properties for a control into four groups: *Format, Data, Event,* and *Other*. By clicking on the appropriate tab, you can view the properties within that category, or you can click the All tab to view all the properties for the control.

The types of properties that are available will vary, depending on the type of control that you are working with. However, in all cases, you can see a detailed explanation of any particular property, using the help screens. Just click inside the row of the desired property in the Property sheet, and press F1 to see a help screen that explains how to use the property in question.

To set a property, in the Property sheet, click in the property whose value you wish to set. If an arrow appears at the right of the property, you can click it and choose a desired value from the list box that opens. If no arrow appears, you can type the desired setting or expression directly into the property box.

Entering Expressions for Calculated Controls

When you add calculated controls, you must enter expressions to display the data you want to appear in the control. You can enter an expression (preceded by an equal symbol) in a text box, and each time a new record is displayed in the form, the expression is re-evaluated. You can enter the expression directly in a text box, using these steps:

1.   Using the Form Tools displayed in the ribbon, add a text box control to the form.

2.   Click once inside the text box, and type an equal (=) symbol.

3.   Type the rest of the needed expression. For example, if the underlying table contained fields named **Bill Rate** and **Hours,** an expression to show the total amount might be as follows:

=[Bill Rate] * [Hours]

4.   Click anywhere outside the text box to complete the entry.

Changing a Form's Background Colors

When manually designing forms, you may want to use background colors that are more visually appealing than the default colors. You can easily change a form's background color using the following steps:

1.   Right-click any blank space in the form.

2.   From the menu that appears, choose Fill/Back Color.

3.   Select the desired color from the pop-up menu that appears.

Dealing with the '#Name?' Error

"When I open my form or report, I see '#Name' in some controls. What happened to my data?"

The above question happens to be the number one question asked of technicians working the Microsoft Access help desks in larger companies around the world, so the question (and its answer) are worth covering here. "#Name" is the error message that appears in a control when Access can't find the data it is supposed to display. Controls are the elements of a form or report that can display data. Each control has many properties that define how it works. The control source property defines the source of the data that the control displays. If this property is set to a source that Access cannot find or that does not exist, you see this error message instead of the data you expect.

The first place that you may want to look when you see this error is in the property sheet for the form or report. Open the form or report in design view, display the property sheet, and click the Data tab. Examine the entry in the control source property. The current setting may be a mistyped field name, or it may refer to a field that was removed from the underlying table or query. Set the property to an existing source of data. After you fix the entry, your form or report should work correctly.

Adding Command Buttons to Forms

Access provides a Command Button Wizard that helps you add command buttons to forms to perform common tasks, such as adding new records, deleting records, or printing the current record displayed in the form. Command buttons can make your forms easier to use, particularly for users who may not be familiar with Access. As an example, the following figure shows a form containing command buttons used for common database tasks.

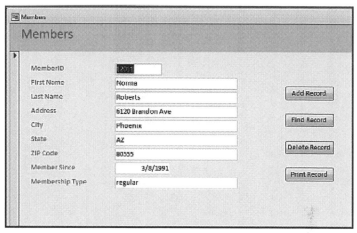

A form containing command buttons

Table 4-1 shows the types of tasks that can be performed with command buttons added using the Command Button Wizards.

You can add a command button to a form with the aid of the Command Button Wizards, by using the following steps:

    1.   If the form tools are not already visible in the ribbon, click the Design tab to display them.

    2.   Click the Command Button tool in the ribbon.

    3.   Click in the form at the location where you want to place the command button.

    4.   Follow the directions that appear in the Command Button Wizard dialog boxes to finish adding the button.

Table 4-1 – Available command buttons

Available categories	When button is pressed, this happens:
Record Navigation	Go to next record Go to previous record Go to first record Go to last record Find Record Go to New Record Find Next
Record Operations	Add New Record Delete Record Duplicate Record Print Record Save Record Undo Record
Form Operations	Apply Form Filter Close Form Edit Form Filter Open Form Print Form Print Current Form Refresh Form Data
Report Operations	Mail Report Print Report Preview Report Send Report to File
Application	Quit Application Run Application Run MS Excel Run MS Word

	Run Notepad
Miscellaneous	Auto Dialer
	Print Table
	Run Macro
	Run Query

Adding Graphics to Forms

You can easily include graphics or pictures in your forms as design elements. Graphics often serve as decorative elements in forms; some of the backgrounds added by the Form Wizards make use of graphic elements. The following figure shows a form that contains a graphic as a design element.

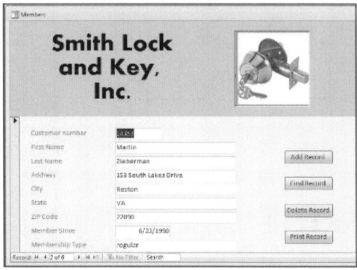

A form containing a graphic

Technically, you could use the Insert Image tool on the ribbon to insert an object frame and place the graphic inside that object frame. However, if all you need is a graphic, it is often easier to just paste in the graphic from another Windows application. When you paste in a graphic that you copy from another Windows program into a form in Design view, the graphic automatically appears in an image frame, and you can move or size the frame as desired. Use the following steps to paste a graphic into a form as a design element:

1. Open the form in Design view.

2. Switch to the graphics program you are using under Windows, and open the file containing the desired graphic.

3. Using the selection techniques appropriate for the graphics program you are using, select the desired portion of the graphic image.

4. From the menus, choose Edit/Copy, to copy the graphic to the Windows Clipboard.

5. Use the Windows Taskbar to switch back to Access.

6. Right-click in the section of the form where you want the graphic to appear, and choose Paste from the menu that appears.

7. Use the moving and sizing techniques covered earlier in this chapter to size the graphic and place it in the desired location in a form.

Saving and Using the Form

You can save a form with the same techniques you use to save objects elsewhere in Access. Click the Save icon at the top left corner of the window, or double-click the form's Close box and answer Yes when asked if you want to save the changes. If you are saving a form for the first time, Access will also ask you for a name for the form. Once saved, the form appears with all other forms in the Forms section of the Navigation pane.

To use the form, you can open it by right-clicking the desired form in the Navigation pane and choosing Open from the menu that appears, or by double-clicking the form in the Navigation pane. Using either method, the form opens in Form view, and you can view or edit data.

As you add records using a form, many of the techniques that you use are the same as you use for adding data through a table's datasheet. Move to the blank record that exists at the end of any table, and enter the data (you can use the navigation buttons at the bottom of the form, or you can use the Go To options listed in the Find area of the ribbon when the form is displayed in form view.)

When you are editing data, you can use the Tab or Shift-Tab keys to move between fields, and you can use the Pg Up and Pg Dn keys to move between records. You can also click in the 'Search' box at the bottom of the form, enter a search string, and press Enter to search for a record containing that term.

Using Filter By Form

Access offers a feature known as "Filter by Form" that you can use to limit the data viewed in forms to meet certain criteria. If you've already learned about queries, you can think of Filter by Form as a way to assign a form query-like properties on the fly. For example, if you were viewing a table of store employees in a form from a personnel database, you could use Filter by Form to limit the form so that only cashiers or only stock clerks were visible in the form. Here are the steps you use to make use of the Filter by Form feature of Access:

1.   With the form open in Form view, click the Advanced drop-down in the 'Sort and Filter' portion of the ribbon, then choose 'Filter by Form' from the menu that appears. In a moment, the form reappears with no data in the fields.

2.   Type criteria that will limit the records into the appropriate fields of the form. For example, if a form contained a field for Employee Title and you only wanted to see cashiers, you would type the word **cashier** into the Employee Type field. You can enter multiple criteria using the words *And* and *Or*; for example, entering **associate or manager** in the Employee Type field filters the form to display associates or managers.

3.   Once you have entered the desired criteria, click the Advanced drop-down in the 'Sort and Filter' portion of the ribbon and choose 'Apply Filter / Sort' from the menu that appears. The filtered records appear in the form, and the word "filtered" appears at the bottom of the form, informing you that a filter applies to the records you are viewing.

The filter remains in effect, until you close the form or remove the filter. To remove the filter, click the Advanced drop-down and choose 'Clear All Filters' from the menu that appears.

TIP: Filters can be saved as part of the form. If you apply a filter to a form and then click the Save button on the toolbar or choose File/Save, Access saves the filter as part of the form.

Creating Relational Forms Manually

Earlier in the chapter, you learned that you can use the Form Wizards to create *relational forms*, or forms that can be used to view data from more than one table (or query) at a time. While the Form Wizards provide the easiest way to create relational forms, you can also create relational forms manually. There are a number of ways to do this in Access. One common method is to use a *main form* which contains the data from the parent table, and add a *subform* which contains the related data from the "child" table in the relationship. The following figure shows an example of a relational form.

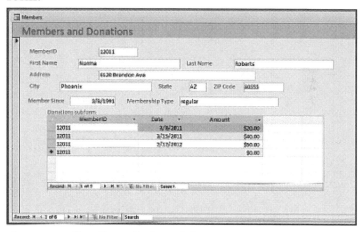

An example of a relational form

If you want to create a relational form manually, you can use the following steps to do this:

1.   Open the main form containing the primary or "parent" data in Design view.

2.   If the various Form Design tools aren't already visible in the ribbon, click the Design tab under Form Design Tools to make them visible.

3.   In the center portion of the toolbar, click the 'More' drop-down arrow just to the left of the 'Insert Image' button (see illustration).

151

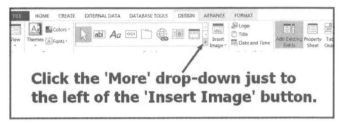

Click the 'More' drop-down just to the left of the 'Insert Image' button.

When you click the arrow, the list of possible tools will open, as shown in the following illustration.

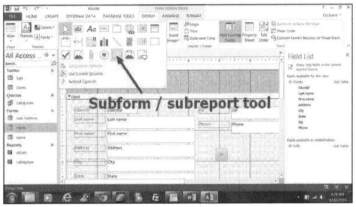

Subform / subreport tool

4. In the third row of tools that appears, click the Subform / Subreport tool (see above illustration).

5. Click and drag in an area of the form where you want to place the subform. When you release the mouse button, a Subform Wizard dialog box will appear, as shown in the following illustration.

152

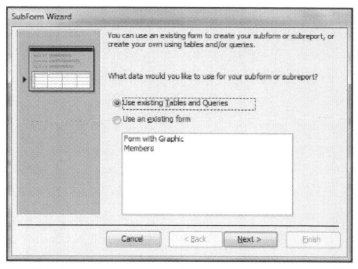

6. Click Next, and choose the table or query that will provide the related records in the dialog box that appears.

7. Click Next, and answer the remaining questions asked by the wizard. Depending on whether relationships have been established at the table level previously, you may be asked which field should be used to link the records shown in the subform to the record in the parent, or main, form.

8. When done adding the subform, select the main form (you can simply click the upper-left corner of the form to select it), and save the form by clicking the Save icon at the upper left. You can then switch to form view to examine the results.

153

A relational form in design view

Access will automatically establish the proper link needed between the primary form and the subform, if you established relationships between the tables being used at the table level as described in Chapter 2. Access will also establish a link if both the main form and the subform use a table that has a matching field (a field with the same field name, and the same field type). If Access cannot establish a link, the Link Master Fields property of the subform's property sheet will be blank, and you will need to fill in the name of the field for the form to operate correctly.

Solving Possible Problems with Relational Forms

If you design a relational form and when you switch to form view you don't see the data you want, the difficulty may be that Access cannot determine how the underlying data should be used in the form. Assuming you are using the form to show records from two tables having a "one-to-many" relationship (one record in the parent table being related to many records in the child table), make sure that the main form uses the parent table as its data source and the subform uses the child table as its data source. Keep in mind that the tables you are using to provide data to the main form and the subform must have a common

154

field that serves to establish the relational link between the tables.

Design tips for relational forms and reports

You should keep in mind some overall design tips when you are designing relational forms and reports.

Keep in mind of the size limitations of the subform or subreport. Because you need to fit a form within a form or a report within a report, you will want to be as efficient as possible with the use of space in your subforms and subreports. Include only those fields that are necessary, and consider using datasheet view for subforms to allow as many fields is possible to fit in the subform.

Don't duplicate main form and report controls in the subform or subreport. Controls that are already present in the main form or report generally serve no useful purpose when they appear again in the subform or subreport. Because the subform or subreport repeats the contents of a control for each record, any control that contains the entries from the common (linking) fields should be placed in the main form or main report, rather than in the subform or subreport.

Avoid page breaks or page numbers in subreports, and remove unneeded headers and footers. You usually do not want to insert a forced page break inside a subreport, and you usually do not need headers and footers, because typically the main report has its own headers and footers.

Protect referential integrity by locking fields in forms if necessary. If you didn't protect referential integrity at the database level, you should definitely do it during the form design process by locking any fields in the subform which, if edited, will break the link between the master record and a detail record.

Summary

In this chapter, you learned how you can create a variety of forms, to use to view and edit your data in Access tables. You learned that you can create forms quickly with the Form option on the ribbon, with the Form Wizards, or by manually designing forms. You also learned how to work with filter by form and how to design and use relational forms. The next chapter will provide specifics on creating and using reports, to provide printed summaries of your data.

You also learned that forms can be based upon queries, and this technique lets you create forms that have a very focused view of specific records, certain fields, or both. The next chapter will provide specifics on creating and using reports, to provide printed summaries of your data.

Chapter 5 - Creating and Using Access Reports

This chapter teaches you how to create and use reports, which in most cases represent the end result of all your work in Access. You use reports to produce, on paper, listings of your data in virtually any conceivable format. Access can provide reports in a wide variety of formats, with varying levels of detail. You can include graphic elements or photographs stored in a table in your reports. And you can easily create reports formatted as mailing labels, to match a variety of popular label sizes. The figure that follows shows an example of a report in Access.

An example of an Access report

As with forms, Access provides three overall methods for producing reports. You can use the Report option of Access to produce a report that is based on a single table or query in a matter of seconds. Or you can use the Report Wizards to quickly design a variety of different types of reports. (Like the Form Wizards, the Report Wizards ask you a series of questions about the design that you prefer, and produce a finished result based on your answers to these questions.) And

157

finally, you can design reports manually, maintaining complete control over the design process.

Plan First, Create Later

When faced with the need to get data from the database onto a printed page, too many Access users leap directly into creating a report, with little or no forethought devoted to the planning process. Some time spent in planning the report can save wasted effort later, especially if the rush to produce the report simply means that you must re-create it later when the departmental manager complains that the report isn't what he or she really wanted. Before starting to create a report in Access, it is often a wise idea to lay out the report on paper, by creating a hand-drawn sketch. You may want to get the opinions of those who will receive the reports during this 'conceptual design' process, to reduce the chances of omitting needed information from the eventual report.

Once you have an idea of the overall format your report should take, you should next create and test the queries that will supply the data to the report. (In theory the report might be based on a table rather than on a query. But in practice, rarely is every single record in a table wanted in a report, so you will probably need queries that sort and select the desired data.)

Finally, with the report's overall design planned and the underlying queries created in Access, you can proceed to create the actual report. You can do this quickly with the assistance of the Report Wizards, or you can manually design the report, placing the desired text boxes, labels, and other design elements at the desired locations within the report.

Creating a Report with the ribbon's Report Option

If you want to create a report that is based on a single table or query, the simplest way to do this is to use the Report option on the Ribbon. The Report option creates a simple tabular report for whatever table or query is selected in the navigation pane when you click the button. To create a report using the Report option, perform these steps:

1. Select the desired table or query to be used as a source of data for the report in the navigation pane. (You don't need to open the table or query; just make sure it is highlighted in the navigation pane.)

2. Click the Create tab, then in the Reports group on the ribbon, click Report. In a moment, Access builds a default report for the table or query; an example of such a report was shown earlier, at the start of this chapter.

NOTE: When you use the Report option to create a report, you get a report in a default columnar arrangement with the fields laid out from left to right, and the field names are used as the default labels for the fields. (If you want to change any of these design aspects of the report, you can easily do so by opening the report in Design view, and making changes to the report manually, as detailed later in this chapter.)

Creating a Report with the Report Wizards

When you want a little more control over the end result (or when you need to create a report based on more than one table or query) but you still want Access to help you with the overall process, you can use the Report Wizards to aid in the creation of your reports. Like all wizards in Access, the Report

Wizards ask you a series of questions and produce a finished, ready-to-use object (in this case, a report) based on your answers to the questions.

The steps listed below are the overall steps you will use to create reports with the Report Wizards. The paragraphs that follow these steps describe the steps in greater detail.

1. Click the Create tab in the ribbon.
2. In the Reports group of the ribbon, click Report Wizard.
3. Follow the directions and answer the appropriate questions that appear in the wizard dialog boxes. In the last dialog box that appears, click 'Open the report with data in it' then click Finish to begin viewing or printing data in Print Preview, or click 'Modify the report's design' then click Finish to open the report in Design view, where you can make additional changes to the design of the report.

That's the process of using the Report Wizards, in a nutshell. Now, here is the process in greater detail:

When you click the Create tab in the ribbon and then click Report Wizard, the first dialog box for the Report Wizards appears, as shown here.

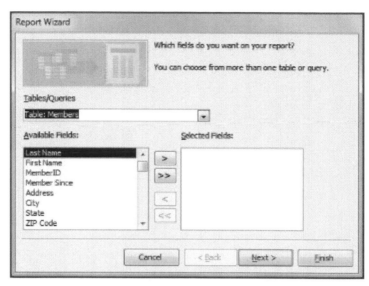

Initial dialog box for Report Wizards

Choosing the Tables and the Desired Fields

At the top of the dialog box is a Tables/Queries list
box. As you select a desired table or query from this
list, the fields in that table or query appear below, in
the Available Fields portion of the dialog box. You
can click on any field to select it, then click the Right
Arrow button to add the field to the Selected Fields
list at the right side of the dialog box. (Alternately,
you can double-click any field in the Available Fields
list box, to add it to the Selected Fields list box.) If
you want to include all the fields in the table or query
in the report, just click the double right-arrow button.
If you make a mistake and add a field you don't want
in the report, select it in the Selected Fields list box,
then click the left arrow button to remove that field
from the list.

If you want to create a *relational report* (a report that
is based on more than one table or query), first add all
the desired fields from the first table (or query). Then
choose another table (or query) in the Tables/Queries
list box, and add the desired fields for that table or

161

query. Once you have finished adding all the fields needed by your report, click Next.

The dialog box that appears next depends on whether you have chosen fields from a single table or query, or from more than one table or query. If you are using the Report Wizard to create a report based on multiple tables and/or queries, the next dialog box that you see is the one shown in the figure that follows. The left side of this dialog box asks you how you want to view the data, and it provides a list of the tables or queries you have chosen earlier to provide the data to the report. In effect, you are deciding which table (or query) should be the *parent data source*, or the table or query with the highest priority. Make a selection by clicking the desired table or query in the list at the left side of the dialog box, then click Next.

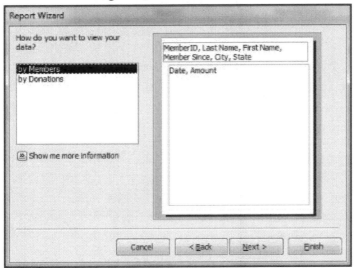

Second Report Wizard dialog box (used for multiple tables)

Once you make your selection (or, if you originally selected fields from only one table or query) you next see the Report Wizard dialog box shown here.

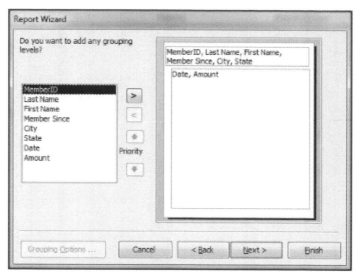

The Report Wizard dialog box used for grouping

You can use the options shown in this dialog box to specify levels of *grouping*, if desired, for the report. To specify grouping levels, select a desired field to base the groups of records on, then click the right-arrow button to add a group band for that field. (Each group band that you add denotes a section within the report where the records will appear by groups.) After choosing any desired grouping, click Next to proceed. Or, if you don't want any grouping in the report, you can click Next without selecting any fields in the dialog box. (For more specifics about grouping, see "Adding Sorting and Grouping to a Report" later in this chapter.)

The next dialog box that appears (see below) asks you to choose a sort order for the detail records that will appear in the report. You can sort on up to four fields when using the wizards to create a report. When sorting on multiple fields, the first field that you choose has the highest priority in the sort, the second field has the second-highest priority, and so on. Make any desired selections in the dialog box, and click Next. (Note that if you need to sort a report on more than four fields, you can manually modify the sorting for the report; see "Adding Sorting and Grouping to a Report" later in this chapter for details.)

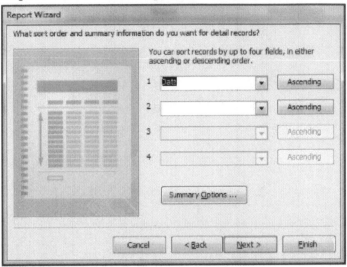

The Report Wizard dialog box used for establishing a sort order

The next dialog box to appear (see below) asks you to select the desired layout for the report, and it lets you choose a desired orientation (portrait or landscape). You can also turn on an option that lets Access automatically adjust field widths to fit all fields on a single page. Make your desired selections in the dialog box, then click Next.

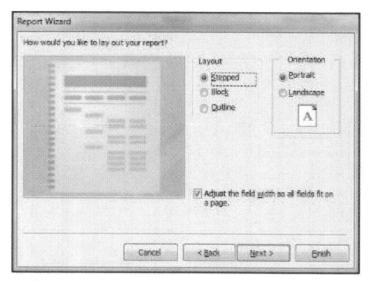

The Report Wizard dialog box used for layout and orientation

Completing the Design Process

The last dialog box that appears, shown below, asks for a title for the report. A default title is provided (which is the same as the primary table or query that the report was based upon), and you can leave this title, or change it to any title you wish.

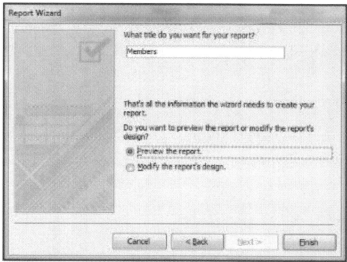

Last dialog box for Report Wizards

Additionally, the options in the final dialog box let you open the report in Print Preview mode (where you can see how the report will appear or print the report), or open the report in 'Design view' where you can make further modifications to the design of the report. Once you click Finish, the Report Wizard completes the process of creating the report.

Once the report has been saved, it appears in the navigation pane under the Reports section, and you can double-click it or right-click it and choose Open from the shortcut menu, to open the report in Print Preview mode, or you can right-click the report and choose Print from the menu to print the report. For more details on previewing and printing reports, see "Previewing a Report" or "Saving and Printing the Report" later in this chapter.

Designing Reports Manually? Let the Report Wizards Lend a Hand!

In some cases you may prefer to design your own reports. However, you shouldn't ignore the helpful capabilities of the Report Wizards. You can usually save considerable time and effort by letting the Report Wizards create a report, then you can open that report in Design view, and make manual changes to the report. using the techniques described in the topic that follows.

Designing Reports Manually

If you prefer the "do-it-yourself" method for creating reports (a glutton for punishment, eh?), Access will certainly not stand in your way. You can design your own reports from scratch, using the manual method of report design. With this method, you open a blank report, size the report to the desired width and height, and add the desired *design objects* such as text boxes that display the contents of fields, labels, graphics, lines, and so on, to the report. The overall steps behind the manual creation of reports are as follows:

1. In the ribbon area, click the Create tab.

2. In the Reports area of the ribbon, click the Report Design button to open a new, empty report in the main portion of the window. (An example is shown in the illustration that follows.)

3. Open the Property Sheet for the report, click the Data tab, and choose the table or query that should serve as the primary source of data for the report.

4. Using the Report Design Tools that appear in the ribbon area along with the 'Add Existing Fields' icon in the ribbon, place the desired objects (text boxes, labels, and any other types of controls that are needed) on the report.

5. Click the Save icon at the upper left to save the completed report.

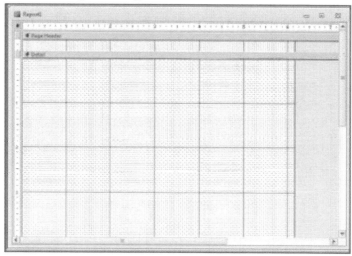

A blank report in Design view

In addition to manually creating reports from scratch, you can also open existing reports that have been created with the Report option or with the Report Wizards in Design view. To do so, right-click the report's name in the Navigation pane, and choose Design View from the menu that appears. The following figure shows an example of an existing report, created using the Report Wizards, that has been opened in Design View.

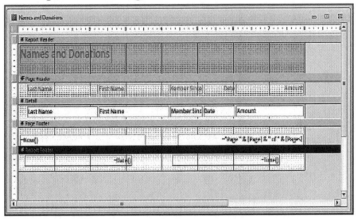

An existing report open in Design view

Existing reports will usually contain *text box controls*, which are used to display the data contained in the fields of the table or query. Reports also typically contain *label controls*, which provide the user with feedback about the various objects on the report, or about how to interpret the data contained within the report. Optionally, reports can contain report headers and report footers.

Understanding a Report's Layout

A report's layout contains a number of different sections called *bands;* these are illustrated in the figure that follows. Understanding how these bands are used, and how they relate to each other is vital in designing effective reports.

By default, a new report that you create contains a *page header band*, a *page footer band*, and a *detail band*. Optionally, reports can also contain *report header bands* and *report footer bands*, and they can contain *group bands*. These parts of a report are shown in the illustration on the following page, and the purpose of each of the bands are detailed after the illustration.

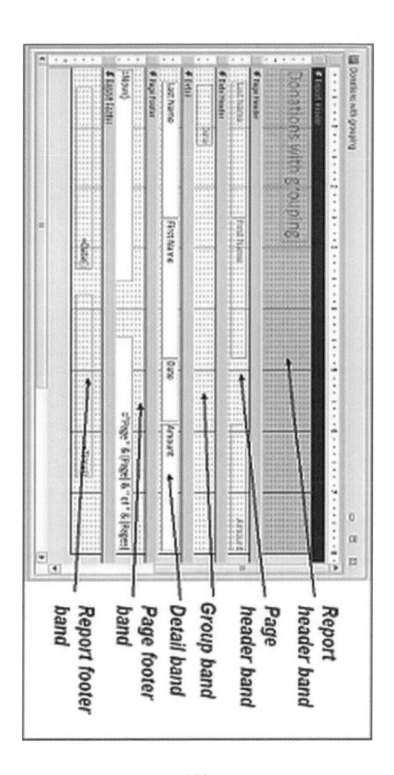

Report
header band

Page
header band

Group band

Detail band

Page footer
band

Report footer
band

170

Report header bands contain information that appears once, at the beginning of the report. (Typically, the title of the report is placed in this area.) *Report footer bands* contain information that appears once, at the end of the report. (Many financial reports include summary fields that provide numeric or currency totals in the report footer band.) If a report does not contain report header and footer bands, you can add them while in Design view by choosing View/Report Header/Footer.

Page header bands appear at the top of each page. If the report includes a report header band, the page header band on the first page of the report will appear directly beneath the report header band. With reports that are tabular in nature, the page header band typically contains field names corresponding to the columns of data that will appear underneath. *Page footer bands* appear at the bottom of each page. (Page numbers are usually placed in the page footer band.) If the report includes a report footer band, the page footer band on the last page of the report appears directly above the report footer band. If a report does not contain page header and footer bands, you can add them while in Design view by choosing View/Page Header/Footer.

The *Detail band* contains the actual data that appears in the body of the report. The detail band appears on each page, sandwiched between any page header band and page footer band. Text boxes that contain the contents of the fields from the underlying table or query are typically placed in the detail band.

Group bands, which are optional, appear once for each group of records. When you use group bands, a *group header band* appears above the detail records for the group, and a *group footer band* appears below the detail records for the group. Group bands, when used, typically contain labels or text boxes that serve to identify the group. As an example, if a general contractor's report of hours worked on multiple job sites contained records of time entries by sucontractor and job worked by the subcontractor, you would probably want to group the records by individual subcontractor, and within each subcontractor grouping, by job number.

When Access prepares a report for printing, it begins by printing the contents of the report header band, followed by the contents of the page header band. Then Access prints detail sections until the bottom of the page is reached. Access then prints the contents of the page footer band, then sends a page break to the printer to feed the next sheet of paper. Access then prints the contents of the page header band, followed by another detail section, followed by the page footer band and another page break. On the final page of the report, Access follows the same sequence, adding the contents of the report footer band at the end of the report.

The process of printing a report is basically the same when your report includes group bands, with the following exception. Access prints the contents of the group header band before the first record in each group, and it prints the contents of the group footer band after the last record in each group.

It is important to understand where Access prints each band, because a thorough knowledge of the purpose of each band will ensure that you place the desired controls in the correct bands when designing your reports. For example, if you wanted to place a text title at the top of the first page, you would need to put a label containing the text in the report header band. However, if you wanted that title to appear at the top of every page, you would place the label in the page header band, rather than in the report header band.

Working with the Design Surface

When you create a report manually, it initially opens to a default size, occupying the active window. Rulers appear at the top and left edges of the report, and a grid composed of dots fills the drawing area by default. You can change the size of the report as necessary, to accommodate as many fields or other objects as you may need. Use the following steps to change the size of a report:

1. While in Design view, place the pointer on the bottom edge or right edge of the report. The pointer changes to a double-headed arrow.

2. Drag the pointer up or down to change the height of the report, or drag the pointer left or right to change the width of the report.

Adding Controls to Reports

As you design reports, most objects you add to the report (such as labels, and text boxes that display fields) are called *controls*. If you are going to do much work with reports in Design view, you must know how to add controls, move them, and size them as needed. Many of the same techniques used in report design are also used when manually designing forms. In Access, you can add three types of controls to reports (or to forms). They are *bound controls, unbound controls,* and *calculated controls.*

- **Bound controls-** These are controls that are connected to a field of the table or query that the report is based upon. In the figure shown previously, the text boxes that display the contents of the fields are bound controls. The most commonly-used type of bound control is the text box control. However, other types of bound controls can also be used in reports, such as check boxes, list boxes, and object

173

frames (which, in reports, typically display photos stored in OLE fields of a table).

- *Unbound controls-* These are controls that are not connected to any fields of a table or query. In reports created by the Report Wizards, the title that appears in the report header and the labels containing the names of the fields are unbound controls.

- *Calculated controls-* These are controls that display the results of a calculation. The expression used to perform the calculation is typically based on one or more fields of a table.

You add controls to reports using the variety of tools that appear in the ribbon area when you have a report open in Design View. These tools are shown in the illustration on the page that follows.

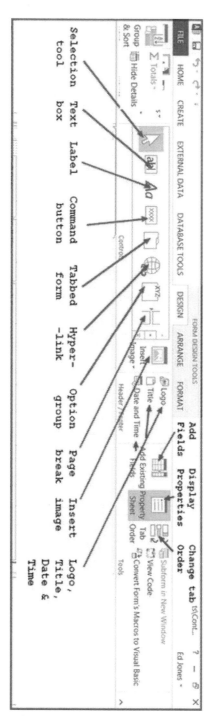

The tools used for Report Design

175

When you want to add bound controls to a report, the easiest way to do so is to use the Field List. Click the Add Existing Fields button near the right side of the ribbon, and choose the table or query from the list that appears at the right. Once you select a table or query, a list of fields from that table or query will be displayed.

Assuming the type of control you want to create is a text box, you just drag the desired field from the Field List to the desired location on the report. When you release the mouse button, a text box bound to the appropriate field appears.

You can add multiple fields to the report as text boxes in a single operation, by selecting the first field in the Field List, then holding the Ctrl key as you select each additional desired field in the list. Once all the needed fields are highlighted, click on any selected field, and drag the fields onto the report as a group. (Note that if the fields are too close together for your liking, you can easily space them apart by clicking the 'Arrange' tab under 'Report Design Tools' in the ribbon, and then using the various options shown under 'Size/Space' in the ribbon.)

To add other types of controls to a report, you use the assortment of tools shown in the previous illustration. The various tools and their uses are described in the list that follows. (***NOTE that some of these tools that you see in the ribbon will not actually apply to reports; they appear because internally, Access uses the same programming to show tools for both forms and for reports.***)

- *Selection tool - Selects, moves, or sizes objects within the report. If another tool was previously selected, clicking the Selection tool deselects that tool.*

- *Text Box - Used to create a text box that displays the contents of a field, or the results*

176

of an expression. Text boxes are usually bound (or tied) to a field in a table or a query.

- *Label - Used to add a label, commonly used as descriptive text, titles, captions, or instructions.*

- *Command Button – These are typically used with forms and not with reports.*

- *Tabbed Control - These are typically used with forms and not with reports*

- *Hyperlink - Used to add a reference to a hyperlink to a report.*

- *Option Group - Used to add option groups. Option groups are used to show two or more option buttons, toggle buttons, or check boxes; only one of the options in an option group will be shown as being selected at a time.*

- *Option Button - Used to add an option button. Option buttons are circles that appear darkened in the center when selected. Option buttons (also culled radio buttons) can be used in an option group to choose a single choice from many, or they can be used individually to specify a yes/no choice.*

- *Page Break - Used to insert a page break into the report. (Page breaks force the start of a new page when a report is printed, but they are not visible when the report is viewed.)*

- *Combo Box - These are typically used with forms and not with reports.*

- *Chart - Used to add a chart to a report. This tool launches a chart wizard, which you use to design a chart based on values in the*

table or query that supplies data to the
report.

- *Line - Used to draw lines in a report.*
(Lines are typically used in reports to
provide a visual separation of other objects.)

- *Toggle Button - These are typically used*
with forms and not with reports.

- *List Box - Used to create a list box. List*
boxes are used to show values from a
predetermined list. The choices in the list are
often based on rows of a query, but they can
also be based on a list of predetermined
values.

- *Rectangle - Used to add rectangles or*
squares to a report.

- *Check Box - Used to add a check box.*
Check boxes are small squares that contain
an 'X' when selected. Check boxes can be
used in an option group to choose a single
choice from many, or they can be used
individually to specify a yes/no choice.

- *Insert Image - Used to add a frame used*
to display a static (unchanging) graphic
image.

To create a label, click the Label tool. On the report, click where you want to place the label, type the text for the label, and press Enter. (You can change the label's font and size, if desired, by selecting it and then choosing the desired font and font size from the font options shown in the ribbon.)

The exact steps for creating other types of controls will depend on the type of control, but here are the overall steps you can use:

1. If the report tools are not already visible in the ribbon, click the Design tab to display them.

2. Click the tool representing the desired type of control you want to create.

3. Click in the report where you want to place the upper-left corner of the control, and drag the pointer to size the control to the desired size. If a wizard is appropriate to the type of control you are adding, you can follow the directions in the Control Wizard dialog boxes that appear.

Moving, Sizing, and Deleting Controls

As you work with controls, you will often want to move them, or change the size of controls. To move a control, first select the control by clicking anywhere within the control. Then move the pointer to any edge of the control where the pointer changes shape to a four-pointed arrow, and drag the control to the desired location.

TIP: You can move a group of controls in one operation, by first selecting the controls as a group. To do this, select the first control, then hold the Shift key as you select each additional desired control. When all the controls are selected, you can move the pointer to any edge of any selected control where the pointer changes shape to a four-pointed arrow, and drag the controls as a group to the desired location.

To resize a control, select the control by clicking on it. Then move the pointer to any of the control's sizing handles (where the pointer changes shape to a four-pointed arrow), and click and drag the control to the desired size.

To move a text box control separately from its label, place the pointer over the handle at the upper-left corner of the text box, where the pointer changes to a four-pointed arrow. Then click and drag the text box to the desired location.

To delete a control that is not wanted, select the control, then press the Del key.

TIP: Occasionally, you will want to move controls very small distances. You can easily do this by selecting the control, then holding the Ctrl key depressed and using the arrow keys.

Changing a Control's Properties

Controls have *properties* that affect how the control behaves when the report is displayed or printed, and you can put these properties to use in designing your reports for ease of use and accurate data entry. To change the properties of a control, first select the control by clicking on it. Then click the Property Sheet button in the ribbon. When you do this, a Property sheet appears at the right for the selected control. The following figure shows the Property sheet for a text box control, the type of control most commonly used both in forms and in reports.

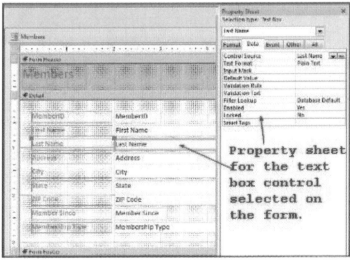

Property sheet for the text box control selected on the form.

***The Property sheet for a text box control (this
example is from a form, but the same control is used
in both forms and reports)***

Notice that the Property Sheet groups properties for a
control into four groups: *Format, Data, Event,* and
Other. By clicking on the appropriate tab, you can
view the properties within that category, or you can
click the All tab to view all the properties for the
control.

The types of properties that are available will vary,
depending on the type of control that you are working
with. However, in all cases, you can see a detailed
explanation of any particular property, using the help
screens. Just click inside the row of the desired
property in the Property sheet, and press F1 to see a
help screen that explains how to use the property in
question.

To set a property, in the Property sheet, click in the
property whose value you wish to set. If an arrow
appears at the right of the property, you can click it
and choose a desired value from the list box that
opens. If no arrow appears, you can type the desired
setting or expression directly into the property box.

Entering Expressions for Calculated Controls

When you add calculated controls, you must enter
expressions to display the data you want to appear in
the control. You can enter an expression (preceded by
an equal symbol) in a text box, and each time a new
record is displayed in the form, the expression is re-
evaluated. You can enter the expression directly in a
text box, using these steps:

1. Using the Report Tools displayed in the
   ribbon, add a text box control to the report.
2. Click once inside the text box, and type an
   equal (=) symbol.

3. Type the rest of the needed expression. For example, if the underlying table contained fields named **Bill Rate** and **Hours**, an expression to show the total amount might be as follows:

=[Bill Rate] * [Hours]

4. Click anywhere outside the text box to complete the entry.

Adding Graphics to Reports

You can easily include graphics or pictures in your reports as design elements. Graphics often serve as decorative elements in reports. Technically, you could use the Image tool of the Toolbox to insert an object frame and place the graphic inside that object frame. However, if all you need is a graphic, it is often easier to just paste in the graphic from another Windows application. When you paste in a graphic that you copy from another Windows program into a report in Design view, the graphic automatically appears in an unbound object frame, and you can move or size the frame as desired. Use the following steps to paste a graphic into a report as a design element:

1. Open the report in Design view.
2. Switch to the graphics program you are using under Windows, and open the file containing the desired graphic.
3. Using the selection techniques appropriate for the graphics program you are using, select the desired portion of the graphic image.
4. From the menus, choose Edit/Copy, to copy the graphic to the Windows Clipboard.
5. Use the Windows Taskbar to switch back to Access.

6. Right-click in a section of the report where you want the graphic to appear, and choose Paste from the shortcut menu that appears.

7. Use the moving and sizing techniques covered earlier in this chapter to size the graphic and place it in the desired location in a report.

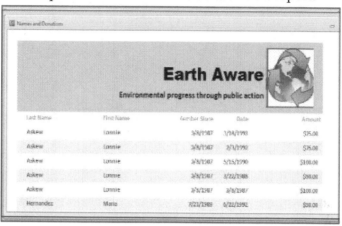

A report containing a graphic

Working with Photos Stored in OLE Object Fields

One common use for OLE Object fields in a table is to allow for the display (and printing) of multiple images, with a separate image stored in each record of a table. The possibilities for such usage of Access are virtually endless; some common examples might include a personnel database that includes a photo of every employee, a web-enabled real estate database that includes listings of homes for sale, or an online sales database used to display items available for purchase. The following figure shows a report based on a table that includes an OLE Object field used to store photos.

A report with photos contained in a table's OLE Object field

When designing the form or the report that you'll use to display or print the photos, you use the same overall design techniques as with any bound control based on a table's field. Drag the field from the Fields list to desired location in the report, then use the sizing techniques described earlier in this chapter to increase the size of the field (as necessary) to show and print the photograph. Depending on your application (and on the size of your photos), you may want to modify the Size Mode property setting for the bound object frame that's used to display or print the photos in the report. The following illustration shows the Size Mode property for the frame used to display the photos in the previous example. Note that you have three possible options: clip, stretch, and zoom.

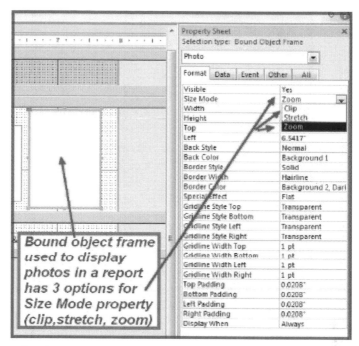

Bound object frame used to display photos in a report has 3 options for Size Mode property (clip,stretch, zoom)

The Size Mode property options for an OLE object field in a report

Clip, which is the default, displays the object at its actual size. If the photo is larger than the control, the image is clipped on the right and bottom by the control's borders. Stretch resizes the object as needed to fill the control. Since this setting changes both height and width as needed to fit the control size, you may see distortion in the photograph. Finally, zoom displays the entire object, resizing it as needed without distorting the proportions of the object. (With the Zoom setting, you may see extra white space in the control if Access must resize the photo.) You will want to take the size of your photos (or other graphics to be displayed) into account, and choose the setting that works best for you.

Previewing the Report

At any time during the design process, you can preview the report to see an on-screen representation of how the report will look when it is printed. To preview a report, chose View>Print Preview from the ribbon, or right-click the report's header, and choose Print Preview. Using either method, a preview of the report appears in a window. You can use the scroll bars or the PgUp and PgDn keys to see additional portions of the report while in preview mode. And you can use the arrows at the bottom of the window to view other pages of the report. The Zoom button in the ribbon of the preview window can be used to enlarge the image that you are viewing, and the Close button can be used to close the preview window when you are done previewing the report.

Saving and Printing Reports

You can save a report with the same techniques you use to save objects elsewhere in Access. Click the Save icon at the upper left, or right-click the report's header bar and choose Save from the popup menu. If you are saving a report for the first time, Access will also ask you for a name for the report. Once saved, the report appears with all other reports in the Reports tab of the Navigation pane.

To print an existing report, highlight the desired report in the Navigation pane, and choose Print. Alternately, you can right-click the report by name, and choose Print from the shortcut menu. With either method, the Print dialog box appears. In the dialog box, you can choose a range of pages, the number of copies to be printed, and the printer to use. Make your desired selections in the dialog box, and click OK to begin printing.

Changing a Report's Data Source

When you initially create a report (whether you use the Report Wizards or design the report manually) you indicate the source of the data by choosing a table or query during the report creation process. That table or query name is saved to the report's *record source* property, so that Access knows where to find the data for the report. Occasionally, you may need to change the record source property for an existing report, so that the report uses a different table or query (of course, the table or query must contain all the fields needed by the report). You can change the record source property for a report using the following steps:

1.   Open the report in Design view.

2.   If the Property Sheet is not already visible, click the Property Sheet icon in the ribbon to display the window.

3.   Click the Data tab in the Properties window.

4.   In the Record Source box, choose the desired query or table that should provide the data to the report.

5.   Save the report.

Adding Sorting and Grouping to Reports

Most reports are designed with the data sorted in a specific order. You can include a sort order in the design of a report. (If a report is based on a query that includes a sort order and no sort order is specified for the report, the records will appear sorted according to the design of the query.)

In addition to sorting, you can also group records by sorted categories. Sorting and grouping work hand in hand, because when you include a sort order in a report, the records appear in groups based on the fields used for the sort. You can control both sorting and grouping in Access reports that you design manually, by means of the Sorting and Grouping Pane. You can add sorting and optionally, grouping (the presence of group bands) to a report with the following steps.

1. Open the report in Design view.

2. In the Grouping and Totals area of the ribbon, click the Group and Sort icon. A Group and Sort pane will appear beneath the report's design, as shown here.

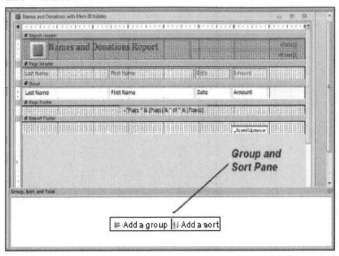

3. Click **Add A Group** to add grouping, or click **Add A Sort** to add sorting. A new line is added to the Group and Sort pane, and a list of available fields appears, as shown here.

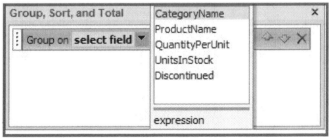

4. Choose the desired field for the group or the sort from the list.

5. Save the report.

If you decide to include a group header band with your report, you will likely want to include the field that identifies the group within the band. (For example, if a report is grouped by Customer ID number, it would make sense to include the Customer ID field in the group header band.) As you make your various selections in the Sorting and Grouping dialog box, remember that you can always visually check the effects of your selections by previewing the report as you make changes to its design.

Adding Page Numbers to a Report

You can easily include the current page number in reports that you design manually. (Reports created with the Report Wizards automatically include page numbers in the design of the reports.) You can add a page number to any report with these steps:

1. Open the report in Design view.

2. In the ribbon, click the Page Numbers icon. The Page Numbers dialog box appears, as shown here.

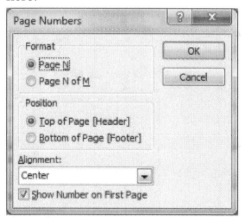

3. Choose the desired format, position, and alignment for the page numbers from the options shown in the dialog box.

4. To include page numbering on the first page of the report, turn on the Show Number on First Page check box.

5. Click OK.

TIP: If for some reason you want to start page numbering of a report with a number other than 1, you will need to use a procedure somewhat different than the one listed above. You must manually add a text box control to the page footer band of the report. Use the text box tool to add a textbox control to the band. Then, click inside the text box, and type the following expression:

=[Page] + *starting number* **- 1**

where *starting number - 1* is a value that is one less than the desired starting page number for the report. For example, if you want the first page of the report to have a page number of 25, you would enter **=[Page] + 24** into the text box.

Adding the Current Date or Time to a Report

You can also easily add the current date or time to a report that you design manually. Here are the steps needed to do so:

1. Open the report in Design view.

2. In the ribbon, click the Date and Time icon. The Date and Time dialog box appears, as shown here.

3.   To include a date, turn on the Include Date option. To include a time, turn on the Include Time option.

4.   Choose the desired date or time format from the available options, then click OK. In a moment, a text box appears in the report containing the expression needed for the date and/or time.

5.   Drag the text box to the desired location in the report.

Creating Mailing Labels

Access provides a Mailing Label Wizard that helps you create reports formatted as mailing labels. You can create reports to produce labels in a variety of formats, including most popular Avery® sizes of labels. The figure that follows shows an example of a report designed to produce mailing labels.

A report designed for producing mailing labels

You can use the following steps to create mailing labels:

1. Select the desired table or query to be used as a source of data for the report in the navigation pane. (You don't need to open the table or query; just make sure it is highlighted in the navigation pane.)

2. Click the Create tab, then in the Reports group on the ribbon, click Labels.

3. In the list box at the bottom of the dialog box, select the table or query that is to provide the data for the mailing labels, and click OK. In a moment, the first Label Wizard dialog box appears, as shown here.

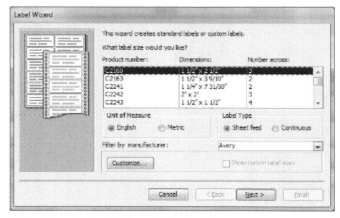

The first Label Wizard dialog box

4. Choose the size and type of label desired, then click Next.

5. In the next Label Wizard dialog box that appears, choose the font and colors desired for the label, then click Next. In a moment, the third Label Wizard dialog box appears (see below), asking which fields should appear on each label.

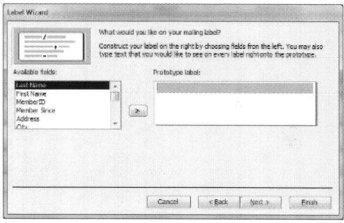

The third Label Wizard dialog box

6. Select the first field that should appear on the first line of the label, then click the > button to place that field in the Prototype Label list box at the right side of the dialog box.

193

7.   To follow the field you just added with any spaces or punctuation, type the spaces or punctuation needed.

8.   To add another field to the same line of the label, select that field in the Available Fields list, then click the > button.

9.   To add a field to the next line of the label, press ENTER, then select the field in the Available Fields list, then click the > button.

10. Repeat steps 6 through 9 for each successive row of the label. As you create the label, the Prototype Label portion of the dialog box shows how the label will appear.

11. When you have added all necessary fields, click Next. In a moment, the fourth Label Wizard dialog box appears (see below), asking how the labels should be sorted.

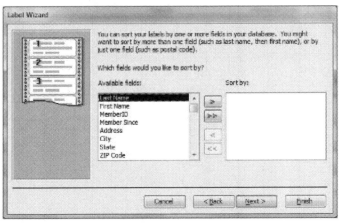

The fourth Label Wizard dialog box

12. Select the field to be used as the highest priority for any sort order, and click the > button.

13. If desired, select the next field to be used in any sort order, and click the > button.

14. Repeat step 13 for each additional field you want to use in the sort order.

15. When done choosing fields for the sort order, click Next. Access will display a final Label Wizard dialog box, asking whether you want to see the labels in preview mode, or modify the labels (open the report in Design view). Make your desired selection in the dialog box, and click Finish.

Once you have completed creating the mailing labels, you can preview or print the labels at any time as you would any other report, by selecting the report in the navigation pane and choosing View>Print Preview from the menus, or by right-clicking the report and choosing Print Preview or Print from the shortcut menu that appears.

Creating Relational Reports

When you need to create relational reports, you can use a very similar process as was described earlier for creating relational forms. Access provides a set of wizards called the Report Wizards, and they operate in a manner very similar to that of the Form Wizards. The steps listed below are the overall steps you can use to create relational reports with the Report Wizards. The paragraphs that follow describe the steps in greater detail.

1. Click the Create tab in the ribbon.
2. In the Reports area of the ribbon, click Report Wizard.
3. Follow the directions and answer the appropriate questions that appear in the wizard dialog boxes. In the last dialog box that appears, click 'Open the report with data in it' then click Finish to begin viewing or printing data in Print Preview, or click 'Modify the report's design' then click Finish to open the report in Design view, where you can make additional changes to the design of the report.

That's the process of using the Report Wizards to create a relational report, in a nutshell. Now, here is the process in greater detail:

When you click the Create tab in the ribbon and then click Report Wizard, the first dialog box for the Report Wizards appears, as shown here.

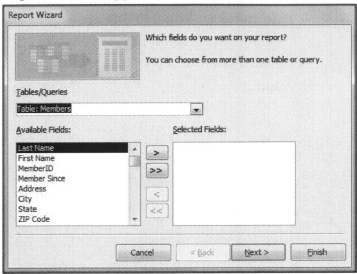

Initial dialog box for Report Wizards

Choosing the Tables and the Desired Fields

At the top of the dialog box is a Tables/Queries list box. As you select a desired table or query from this list, the fields in that table or query appear below, in the Available Fields portion of the dialog box. You can click on any field to select it, then click the Right Arrow button to add the field to the Selected Fields list at the right side of the dialog box. (Alternately, you can double-click any field in the Available Fields list box, to add it to the Selected Fields list box.) If you want to include all the fields in the table or query in the report, just click the double right-arrow button. If you make a mistake and add a field you don't want in the report, select it in the Selected Fields list box, then click the left arrow button to remove that field from the list.

Because you are creating a *relational report* (a report that is based on more than one table or query), you must first add all the desired fields from the first table (or query). Then choose another table (or query) in the Tables/Queries list box, and add the desired fields for that table or query. Once you have finished adding all the fields needed by your report, click Next.

The dialog box that appears next is the one shown in the figure that follows. The left side of this dialog box asks you how you want to view the data, and it provides a list of the tables or queries you have chosen earlier to provide the data to the report. In effect, you are deciding which table (or query) should be the *parent data source*, or the table or query with the highest priority. Make a selection by clicking the desired table or query in the list at the left side of the dialog box, then click Next.

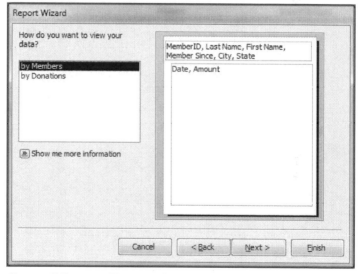

Second Report Wizard dialog box that appears when creating relational reports

Once you make your selection, you next see the Report Wizard dialog box shown here.

197

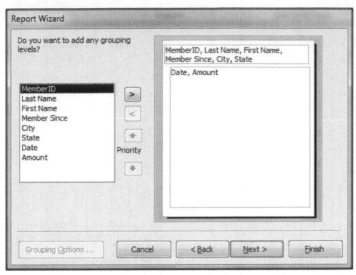

The Report Wizard dialog box used for grouping

You can use the options shown in this dialog box to specify levels of *grouping*, if desired, for the report. To specify grouping levels, select a desired field to base the groups of records on, then click the right-arrow button to add a **group band** for that field. (Each group band that you add denotes a section within the report where the records will appear by groups.)

After choosing any desired grouping, click Next to proceed. Or, if you don't want any grouping in the report, you can click Next without selecting any fields in the dialog box

The next dialog box that appears (see the following illustration) asks you to choose a sort order for the detail records that will appear in the report. You can sort on up to four fields when using the wizards to create a report. When sorting on multiple fields, the first field that you choose has the highest priority in the sort, the second field has the second-highest priority, and so on. Make any desired selections in the dialog box, and click Next.

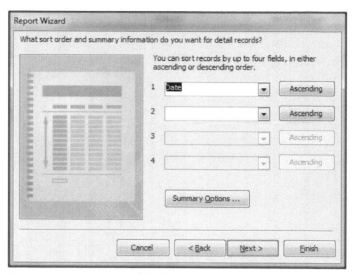

The Report Wizard dialog box used for establishing a sort order

The next dialog box to appear (see the following illustration) asks you to select the desired layout for the report, and it lets you choose a desired orientation (portrait or landscape). You can also turn on an option that lets Access automatically adjust field widths to fit all fields on a single page. Make your desired selections in the dialog box, then click Next.

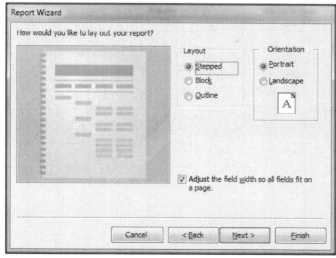

Report Wizard dialog box used for layout

Completing the Design Process

The last dialog box that appears, shown below, asks for a title for the report. A default title is provided (which is the same as the primary table or query that the report was based upon), and you can leave this title, or change it to any title you wish.

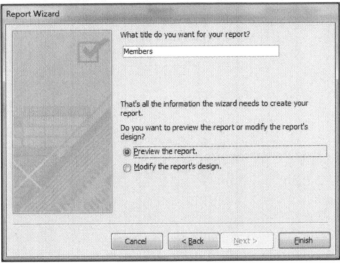

Last dialog box for Report Wizards

Additionally, the options in the final dialog box let you open the report in Print Preview mode (where you can see how the report will appear or print the report), or open the report in 'Design view' where you can make further modifications to the design of the report. Once you click Finish, the Report Wizard completes the process of creating the report.

Once the report has been saved, it appears in the navigation pane under the Reports section, and you can double-click it or right-click it and choose Open from the shortcut menu, to open the report in Print Preview mode, or you can right-click the report and choose Print from the menu to print the report.

Design tips for relational forms and reports

You should keep in mind some overall design tips when you are designing relational reports.

Keep in mind of the size limitations of the subreport. Because you need to fit a report within a report, you will want to be as efficient as possible with the use of space in your subreports. Include only those fields that are necessary.

Don't duplicate main report controls in the subreport. Controls that are in the main report already generally serve no useful purpose when they appear again in the subreport. Because the subreport repeats the contents of a control for each record, any control that contains the entries from the common (linking) fields should be placed in the main report, rather than in the subreport.

Avoid page breaks or page numbers in subreports, and remove unneeded headers and footers. You usually do not want to insert a forced page break inside a subreport, and you usually do not need headers and footers, because typically the main report has its own headers and footers.

Summary

In this chapter, you learned the techniques needed to create reports for your use in Access, whether you create them with the aid of the Report Wizards or by means of the manual report design process. You learned how to create reports that include sorting and grouping, and you learned how to create reports formatted as mailing labels. Using the techniques learned in this chapter and the prior four chapters, you can effectively work with the primary objects needed to do everyday work using Access. The following chapter will show how you can make your work with Access more efficient, by automating repetitive tasks with the help of Access *macros*.

Chapter 6 - Creating and Using Access Macros

This chapter details the use of Access macros. While macros are not as commonly used as the "four basic Access objects" (tables, queries, forms, and reports), macros can prove useful for any tasks that you carry out on a regular basis. In database management software that was popular prior to Microsoft Access (and yes, this author is thinking of "dBase II", having been around for that long!) you could create automated database applications by writing dozens of lines of program code to accomplish specialized tasks. Thankfully, Access will not force you to undergo such torture to automate repetitive tasks. In Access, you can use *macros*, which are groups of instructions, to replace the dozens of lines of program code required by some database programs. When you run the macro, Access carries out the list of instructions.

For example, if on the first workday of each month you must run an append query to copy records to an archive table, followed by a delete query to delete the records from the original table, followed by the printing of a report, you can create a macro that performs all these operations in succession. You could even attach that macro to a command button that you could add to a form. Then, each month instead of spending the first half-hour of every first workday of the month performing all these tasks manually, you could just open the form containing the button, click the button, and have another cup of coffee while Access performs all of these operations in succession. Macros can be considered to be a simple, easy-to-understand way to program in Access. And with the flexibility that has been added to the Macro Builder in Access 2013, you can now manage nearly any task that you might also handle writing program code in

VBA (Visual Basic for Applications). You can think of the Macro Builder as a visual, point-and-click way of programming with Access.

If you are familiar with the way that macros operate in older versions of Microsoft Word and Excel, you should be aware that macros in Access are designed differently than in those products. While many longtime users of Word and Excel are accustomed to creating macros by turning on a "macro recorder" and then performing operations in Word or Excel, you should note that there is no macro recorder in Access. You design macros in Access by choosing the actions that you want to perform from the Macro Builder window.

Introducing the Macro Builder

If you have some experience working with macros in earlier versions of Microsoft Access, you are in for a major change for the better. The old Macro Window that's been around since the first version of Access, with its columns of conditions, actions, and action arguments, has been completely revamped. Access 2013 uses the new Macro Builder shown in the figure that follows. The old grid-based format used in Access versions prior to Access 2010 has been replaced with a more visual design that shows the programming-like abilities of Access macros, as shown in the illustration on the following page.

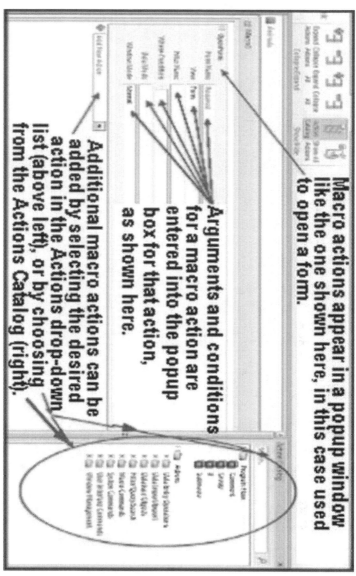

The Macro Builder

In the Macro Builder, conditional statements appear as traditional programming-style "IF" statements, in the center pane of the Macro Builder. And the arguments of each action appear in pop-up windows as a part of each conditional statement, rather than in a list at the

205

bottom of the screen. You add actions to the macro either by selecting the desired action from the Actions drop-down list that appears in the center pane of the Macro Builder, or by choosing the desired action from the Actions Catalog list that occupies the right half of the window.

Once you choose a desired action from the Actions drop-down list, the pop-up window that appears as part of the conditional statement contains arguments and settings that apply to the action you've chosen. You can set these options as desired, to control precisely how the macro performs your chosen tasks.

Creating a Macro

As mentioned, macros are created using the Macro Builder. The precise steps are as varied as the tasks that you want your macros to perform. But the overall steps you will use are the following:

1. Click the Create Tab in the ribbon.

2. Under the 'Macros and Code' section of the ribbon, click Macro to open the Macro Builder.

3. In the 'Add new action' list box in the center pane of the Macro Builder, choose the desired action. For example, if the first action that you want your macro to perform is to open a form in the database, you would choose 'Open Form' from the list.

4. In the pop-up window that now appears for the action you chose, select or fill in the desired options.

TIP: If you want a macro action to open a given table, form, or report or run a query, simply drag the table, query, form, or report from the navigation pane into the center pane of the Macro Builder. The new action will automatically appear representing an open action for that type of object, and you can

then fill in the remaining conditions as desired.

5. Repeat Steps 3 and 4 for all of the actions that you want your macro to perform.

6. Save the macro by clicking the Save icon at the upper-left, or by right-clicking the macro name in the document tab and choosing Save from the shortcut menu that appears.

As an example of a macro, consider the following figure. This particular macro opens a report named 'Animals' in print preview mode, then opens a table named 'Members' in datasheet view. Finally, the macro displays a message box on the screen, indicating to a user that it has completed its assigned tasks.

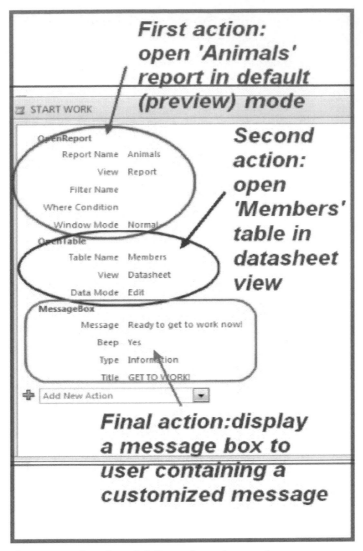

An example of multiple actions in an Access macro

Running Macros

In Access, there are a number of different ways to run a macro. One obvious method is to select the macro in the navigation pane, then on the Database Tools tab of the ribbon, click the Run Macro button. Alternately, you can right-click the macro's name in the navigation pane and choose 'Run' from the menu that appears, or you can double-click the macro in the navigation pane.

You can also run macros by calling them from command buttons that you place on forms. If you open a form in Design view, and drag any existing macro from the navigation pane onto the form, a command button appears. When you switch to Form view and click the button, the macro will run.

Creating a macro that runs whenever a database is opened

One of the most common repetitive tasks that you may want to automate in Access is that of arranging all of your database objects in the manner that you want to see them when you first open the database. You can create a macro that opens all of the desired objects that you normally open when you launch a particular database. Having a macro start automatically each time a database is opened is a simple matter. Simply name the macro with the name 'Autoexec'. Any macro having this name will automatically launch when a database is opened. (if you want to prevent the macro from running at any point in time, simply hold the Shift key depressed as you open the database.)

Typical Uses for Macros

How you design your macros depends entirely on what tasks you want to automate. This will vary widely, depending on your needs. However, here are some common tasks that you can automate using macros:

- Opening and closing a group of forms
- Applying or removing filters or sort orders for forms
- Printing a group of reports

- Running a make-table query to produce a new table, and exporting the new table's data to another file format (such as Excel)
- Importing data from another file (such as a delimited-format file uploaded from an accounting system) into an Access table
- Launching another Windows application automatically from within Access

The best way to determine how you can use macros in your particular work environment is to experiment with the tasks that you perform using Access on a regular basis.

Summary

In this chapter, you learned how to create and run macros. You learned how to create macros that run automatically when a database is opened, and you learned of common uses for macros. In the next chapter, you will learn how you can combine all of the Access objects discussed so far- tables, queries, forms, reports, and macros- into a complete ready-to-use system that other users at your organization can use with little or no specialized training in Access.

Chapter 7 - Creating Custom Applications with Microsoft Access

This chapter is, in effect, a bonus chapter that is included to assist those who desire to do so to move "beyond the basics," so to speak. If you've read through and applied the material in the previous six chapters, you already have an effective knowledge of how you can put Access to work, meeting your needs as a database management system. But, what happens when others in your workplace must share databases that you create for general office use? You may be faced was trying to impart your hard-earned knowledge of Access with each of your coworkers, something that is certain to be a time-consuming task in and of itself. Fortunately, there is an easier way. Using a combination of techniques that you already learned, you can design and implement complete custom applications—database systems that others can use to perform everyday tasks in Access, even if they have little or no familiarity with the program.

This bonus chapter is just one chapter in an entire book about Access application development by this title's author. After using the techniques outlined in this chapter, if you'd like to delve more deeply into this topic, consider purchasing ***Creating Applications with Microsoft Access 2013*** by Edward Jones. You can purchase this book directly from Amazon.

There is no substitute for real-world experience, so the following portion of this article offers a step-by-step example of application development using Access 2013. Before performing the steps, you will need to create two small tables. One, named *Clients*, contains a listing of client names for a sales organization. The second table, named *Calls*, contains a record of each telephone call made by a sales rep to a particular client. Table 1 shows the table structure for the Clients table, with sample data following the design. Table 2 shows the structure for the Calls table, with sample data following the design. A one-to-many relationship exists between the Clients table and the Calls table, as shown in the following figure. (You can use the Relationships button in the Database Tools portion of the ribbon to create this relationship between the tables.)

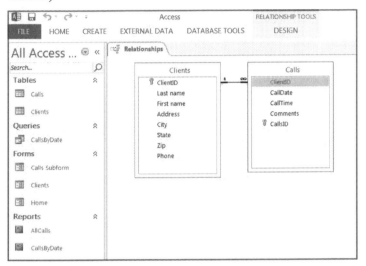

The Relationships window containing the Clients and Calls tables

Creating the database and tables

To get started, launch Access, and choose **File > New** from the menus. When the screen of possible templates appears, Click **Blank Desktop Database.** When prompted for a name, enter **Clients and Calls** as a name, and click **Create**. Once your database exists, you'll want to click the Create tab of the ribbon, then click **Table Design** to begin designing a new table. Specify the following fields for your table:

Table 1 Clients

Field name	Data type
ClientID	AutoNumber (This field should be a key field.)
Last name	Short text
First name	Short text
Address	Short text
City	Short text
State	Short text
Zip	Short text
Phone	Short text

Before saving the Clients table, be sure to designate the ClientID field as a key field, by clicking anywhere within the field in Design View, and clicking the Primary Key icon within the ribbon. After you create the Clients table with the above structure, open the new table in Datasheet view, and enter the following four sample records. (Since you designated the ClientID field as an autonumber field, these values will be entered automatically as you create each record.)

(Sample data for the Clients table:)

Lastname	Smith
Firstname	Linda
Address	101 Main St.
City	Annapolis

State	MD
Zip	20711
Phone	301 555-4032

Lastname	Johnson
Firstname	Steven
Address	452 Apple Way
City	Washington
State	DC
Zip	20005
Phone	202 555-3090

Lastname	O'Malley
Firstname	Susan
Address	1905 Park Ave.
City	New York
State	NY
Zip	10014
Phone	212 555-7879

Lastname	Bannerman
Firstname	David
Address	434 Ocean Dr.
City	Miami
State	FL
Zip	29101

Phone	308 555-2037

The following table shows the fields that you will need in the **Calls** table. Click the Create tab of the ribbon, then click **Table Design** to begin designing another table. Specify the following fields for this table:

(Table 2 - Calls table)

Field name	*Data type*
ClientID	Number
CallDate	Date/time
CallTime	Date/Time
Comments	Long text
CallID	AutoNumber

After you create the Calls table with the above structure, open the new table in Datasheet view, and enter the following five sample records. (Since the CallID field is an AutoNumber field, its value will be filled in automatically as you create the records.)

(Sample data for the Calls table:)

ClientID	1
CallDate	2/15/12
CallTime	9:30 AM
Comments	Schedule shipment of CD101 drives.
CallID	1

ClientID	1
CallDate	2/17/12
CallTime	11:00 AM
Comments	Confirm receipt of CD101 shipment.
CallID	2

ClientID	2
CallDate	2/15/12
CallTime	3:30 PM
Comments	Arrange credit for retail store.
CallID	3

ClientID	4
CallDate	2/16/12
CallTime	10:20 AM
Comments	Customer call re: quality control issues.
CallID	4

ClientID	4
CallDate	2/17/12
CallTime	2:15 PM
Comments	Follow-up to call of 2/16.

CallID	5

Creating the Access Objects

Perform the following steps to create the remaining needed objects for your Access application.

1. Once both tables and the relationship between the tables have been created and the sample records have been added to both tables, in the Navigation Pane at the left, choose Tables, and click Clients to select this table.

2 In the menu bar area (at the top of the screen), click the Create tab. Then under Forms, click Form Wizard to display the Form Wizard dialog box, shown here.

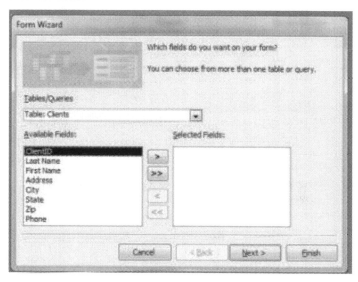

First dialog of the Form Wizard dialog box

3. Click the double-arrow button (>>) to move all the fields from the Clients table into the form. Then under Tables/Queries in the dialog box, open the drop-down and choose Calls. Again, click the double-arrow button (>>) to move all of the

fields from the Calls table onto the form, and click Next.

4. The next screen of the Form Wizard that appears will ask how you want to view the data, by Clients, or by Calls.

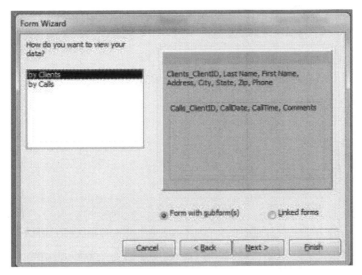

Second dialog of the Form Wizard dialog box

5. Leave the default values as-is, and click Finish. Access will create a default form that displays the clients within the main part of the form, and the calls for each client within a subform, as shown in the illustration on the following page.

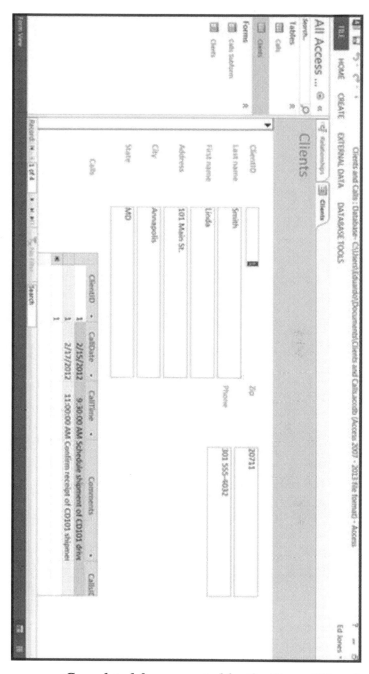

Completed form created by the Form Wizard

6. Right-click the Clients tab for the form (at the top left of the form itself), and choose Design View from the pop-up menu that appears. This action changes the form's appearance from form view to design view.

7. Under the Form Design Tools area now visible in the ribbon, click the Command button icon (the one resembling a rectangle containing a series of letter X's). Then click on a blank space within the right side of the form, to place the button.

8. In the Command Button Wizard dialog box, under Categories, choose **Form Operations**. Under Actions, choose **Close Form**. Click Finish to add a Close button to the form.

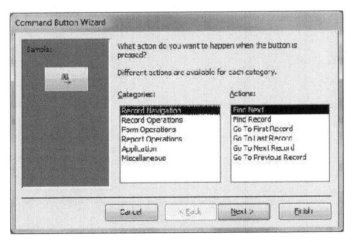

The Command Button Wizard dialog box

9. Save and close the form, and accept the default name of **Clients**.

10. With the Clients table still selected in the Navigation Pane, and the Create tab still active in the ribbon area (at the top of the screen), click Report Wizard. The first dialog box for the Report Wizard appears, as shown in the following figure.

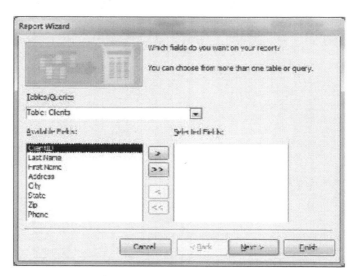

First dialog of the Report Wizard dialog box

11. In the Available Fields portion of the dialog box, double-click the Last Name, First Name, City, and Phone fields.

12. In the Tables/Queries list box within the same dialog box, select the Calls table.

13. In the Available Fields box, double-click the CallDate, CallTime, and Comments fields.

14. In the Report Wizard dialog box, click Finish. Access will create a default report showing each client along with the phone calls made to that client. (In Design View, you may need to widen the CallDate and CallTime fields to get the data to display properly.)

15. Save and close the new report, and in the Navigation Pane, rename the report to **AllCalls**. (To do this, right-click the report in the Navigation Pane, choose Rename from the pop-up menu that appears, and type the new name for the report.)

Next, you will design a *parameter query* that supports the reporting of calls for a range of dates, and you will create a copy of an existing report to be used with the parameter query. Use the following steps to accomplish these design tasks:

1. In the Navigation Pane, under All Access Objects, select Queries.

2. In the ribbon area, under Create, click Query Design.

3. In the Show Table dialog box that appears, double-click both the Calls and Clients tables to add both tables to the design of the query, and click Close to put away the dialog box.

4. In the Clients field list (in the upper portion of the query design window), click the first field to select it, hold the Shift key depressed and click the last field in the list to select all the fields, and click and drag the fields as a group to the first empty column in the query design grid. (You may need to scroll the entire Query Design window upwards to see the horizontal scroll bar.)

5. Scroll to the right within the query design grid and locate the next empty column. Then, in the Calls field list (in the upper portion of the query design window), click the CallDate field, hold the Shift key depressed, and click the Comments field to select the CallDate, CallTime, and Comments fields simultaneously. Then click and drag these fields as a group to the next empty column in the query grid.

6. Locate the CallDate field that was added to the design of the query. In the Criteria row for the CallDate field, type the following expression (including the left and right bracket characters):

Between [Enter starting date:] and [Enter ending date:]

7. Save and close the query. When prompted for a name, call the query **CallsByDate**.

8. In the Navigation Pane, change the object type to Reports, to display the existing reports.

9. Right-click the **AllCalls** report and from the popup menu that appears, choose Copy

10. Right-click in any blank portion of the Navigation Pane, and choose **Paste** from the pop-up menu that appears, to create a copy of the report.

11. When asked for a report name, enter **CallsByDate**.

12. In the Navigation Pane, right-click the CallsByDate report and choose Design to open the CallsByDate report in Design view.

13. If the Properties sheet isn't already visible at the far right, click Property Sheet in the ribbon area to display the Property Sheet for the report.

14. Click the Data tab within the Properties sheet, and widen the right column of the Property Sheet to better see the column's contents.

15. Click the Down Arrow to the right of the Record Source property, and choose CallsByDate from the list. (This action links the new report to the parameter query that you created earlier.)

16. Save the changes to the report, and close the report.

With these objects (two tables, one query, one form with a subform, and two reports) created, you can proceed to create a home screen based on a form that presents a friendly user interface to the end user. As mentioned, home screens are simply blank forms with command buttons added that perform various tasks (such as opening a form or printing a report). The buttons that you place on the blank form can use VBA code (usually added with the aid of the Command Button Wizards) or Access macros to perform common tasks. By way of example, try the following steps to create a home screen for the application:

1. In the ribbon area, under Create, click Blank Form.

2. Right-click the tab of the new form that appears, and choose Design view from the pop-up menu.

3. Using typical Access form design techniques, size the blank form so that it measures roughly four inches square.

4. In the ribbon area, under Form Design Tools, select the Design tab if it isn't already highlighted.

5. In the ribbon area, click the Button icon to select the Command Button tool.

6. Click near the center of the form, roughly one inch below the top of the form to start the Command Button Wizard.

7. Under Categories, choose Form Operations. Under Actions, choose Open Form, and click Next.

8. In the next dialog box that appears, select **Clients** as the form to open, then click Next.

9. In the next dialog box, leave the default choice of 'Open the form and show all the records' selected, and click Next.

10. In the next dialog box, click Text, and enter 'Add or Edit Records' in the text dialog box, then click Finish.

11. In the ribbon area, click the Command Button tool to select it.

12. Click roughly one-half inch below the button you created previously, to start the Command Button Wizard.

13. Under Categories, select Report Operations. Under Actions, select Preview Report, then click Next.

14. In the list that appears in the next dialog box, leave the default of **AllCalls** selected in the list, and click Next.

15. In the next dialog box, click Text, enter 'All Calls Report' in the text box, and then click Finish.

16. In the ribbon area, click the Command Button tool to select it.

17. Click roughly one-half inch below the button you created previously, to start the Command Button Wizard.

18. Under Categories, select Report Operations. Under Actions, select Preview Report, then click Next.

19. In the list that appears in the next dialog box, select **CallsByDate** in the list, and click Next.

20. In the next dialog box, click Text, enter 'Calls by Date Report' in the text box, and then click Finish.

21. In the ribbon area, click the Command Button tool to select it.

22. Click roughly one-half inch below the button you created previously, to start the Command Button Wizard.

24. Under Categories, select Application. Under Actions, leave the default choice of Quit Application selected, and click Next.

25. In the next dialog box, click Text, enter 'Exit System' in the text box, and click Finish.

26. Click above and to the left of the first button, and drag to the lower right of the last button. When you release the mouse, all the buttons should appear selected.

27. Right-click any of the selected buttons and choose Align Left, then right-click any selected button and choose Size/To Widest from the menus.

32. Click the Label tool in the ribbon area, then click and drag near the top of the form to create a new label roughly three inches wide and one-half inch high.

33. Type the heading **Client Calls Tracking System** in the label, and change the font of the label to 16-point type. (You can select the label, then use the Properties Sheet at the far right to change the font.)

34. Click any blank spot in the form to select the entire form. In the ribbon area, click the Property Sheet icon, if it isn't already visible.

35. Click the Format tab of the Property Sheet. In the options that appear, set the Scroll Bars option to Neither, the Record Selectors option to No, the Navigation Buttons option to No, and the Auto Center option to Yes.

36. Save and close the form. When asked for a name, call the form **Home**.

Setting the Database Startup options

Finally, you can set startup options for the database (these are explained in more detail under the heading that follows). Use these steps to do this, completing the design of this simple application:

1. In the main menu bar area at the top of the screen, click the File tab.

2. In the available menu choices, click Options.

3. In the Access Options dialog box that appears (shown below), click Current Database.

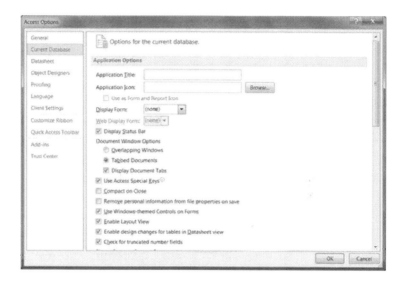

The Access Options dialog box

4. In the Display Form drop-down, choose Home as the screen you want the application to initially display.

5. Turn off the option to Display Navigation Panel, then click OK.

6. Choose File > Close Database to close the database

At this point, the simple application is complete. If you close the database and re-open it, the home screen appears, similar to the example shown in the following figure. From here, users can perform common database tasks with little or no specific knowledge of Microsoft Access.

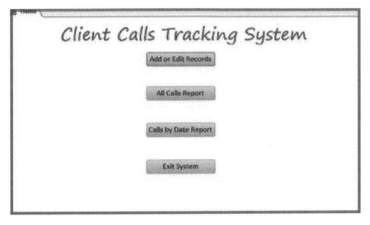

The example home screen

While this example has been kept intentionally simple for the sake of brevity, you can utilize the same techniques with any custom Access application. If your application has a variety of forms and reports (as most do), you can have one form open another from to keep the user interface manageable. For example, a 'Reports' button on your home screen might open another form that contains buttons used to print a variety of reports.

Summary

This chapter has provided an introduction to complete custom applications development using Microsoft Access. And as mentioned at the start of this chapter, the chapter is just one of many chapters in an entire book about Access application development by this title's author. After using the techniques outlined in this chapter, if you'd like to delve more deeply into this topic, consider purchasing ***Creating Applications with Microsoft Access 2013*** by Edward Jones. This advanced text will help you learn to-

•Design tables and relationships for maximum effectiveness
•Learn the secrets of parameter query design to get the data you need on demand
•Design forms and reports with a streamlined user interface that maximizes efficiency and minimizes the chance of data-entry errors
•Put it all together by creating complete applications that others can use with no specialized Access training

Creating Applications with Microsoft Access 2013 is a get-it-done guide for developing complete custom applications using Microsoft Access. If you are a power user who serves as the 'office guru' for everyday users of Access, or a developer for a corporate or government agency who must gain a familiarity with Access as a development platform for applications, you'll find this book to be a must-read. At te Amazon website, perform a search on the title *'Creating Applications with Microsoft Access 2013'* by Edward Jones for additional details.

Chapter 8 - Getting Data In and Out of Access

As a common saying states, "no man is an island," and much the same could be said about computers. Different systems that people work with on an everyday basis utilize a wide variety of different data formats, and it's often necessary to move data between different software programs. Microsoft Access is no slouch in this area. Access was designed from the ground up as having the ability to share data between an Access database and other programs or systems. In fact, when the very first version of Access was under development by Microsoft over two decades ago, Microsoft originally came up with the name "Access" to emphasize the fact that the program had an uncanny ability to work with other software using a variety of different data formats. And over the years, capabilities have been added to Access—so many that it becomes difficult to describe all the ways in which Access can share data with other programs. Here are just a few of the more popular:

- Access can import data from other programs like Excel, Word, Outlook, Open Office, GoogleDocs, and high end database servers like Microsoft SQL Server, Oracle, and Sybase.

- Access can export data to other programs like Word, Excel, Outlook, Open Office, and GoogleDocs.

- Access can be used as a transfer conduit, or a way to move data from one program to another.

- Access can link to other data sources, such as Excel or other Access databases, Microsoft SQL Server databases, or Oracle databases.

You can get a visual idea of the flexibility of Access when it comes to sharing data by looking at the various options on the External Data tab of the ribbon. Open any database and click the External Data tab, and you will see all of the various options used for importing, exporting, and linking to data, as are shown in the illustration on the following page.

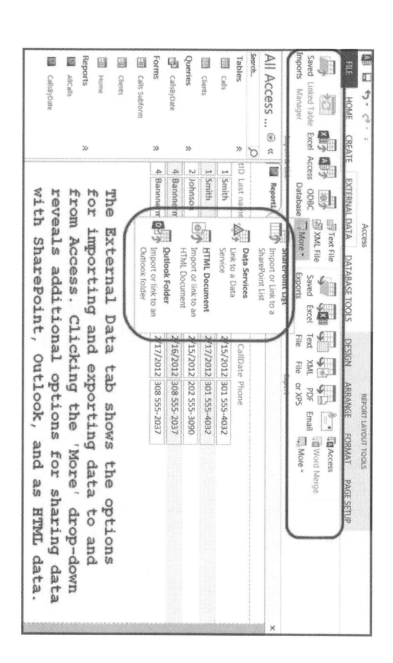

The External Data tab shows the options for importing and exporting data to and from Access. Clicking the 'More' drop-down reveals additional options for sharing data with SharePoint, Outlook, and as HTML data.

233

When it comes to importing and exporting data from Access, your most common tasks by far include moving data to and from Excel, moving data to and from Microsoft Word, and linking to a variety of data sources (often stored on mainframes or other generally less than compatible systems such as Oracle or Sybase database servers). What follows are general instructions for all three of these scenarios.

The Fastest Methods for Moving Data to Excel or Word: Copy and Paste

If you are moving tabular data from a Microsoft Access table into Microsoft Excel or Microsoft Word, the fastest method used is also the easiest by design: a simple copy and paste operation can be used to move a table in Access to a Word table, or to an Excel workbook.

To move the data out of Access using a copy-and-paste operation, first open the desired table in datasheet view. Click the row and column intersection at the upper-left corner of the table, so that the entire table is selected, then right-click at the same upper-left corner and choose Copy from the shortcut menu that appears, to copy the Access table into Windows clipboard memory. Open an Excel spreadsheet or a Word document, and place the insertion pointer where you would like the data to appear. Choose Edit>Paste from the menus, and the data will appear as rows and columns of an Excel worksheet, or as a Word table.

Exporting Access to Word

You can more selectively export data from Access to Word with the following steps:

Open the desired database, and in the navigation pane, select the object that contains the data you want to export. (You can export a table, query, form, or report from Access to Word.)

If you want to export just some of the data from an object, select only those records that should be exported.

With the desired object still highlighted in the navigation pane, click the External Data tab.

In the Export group of the ribbon, click Word.

When prompted, specify the name of the destination file, and click OK. Access exports the data and opens the destination document in Word, depending on the export options you chose in the wizard. Access also shows the status of the operation on the final page of the wizard.

Exporting Access to Excel

Open the desired database, and in the Navigation Pane, select the object that contains the data you want to export. (You can export a table, query, form, or report from Access to Word.)

On the External Data tab, in the Export group, click Excel.

In the Export - Excel Spreadsheet dialog box, you can change the suggested file name for the Excel workbook, if desired. (By default, Access assigns a filename that is the same as the source object).

In the File Format box, choose the file format that matches your version of Excel.

If you are exporting a table or a query, and you want to export formatted data, select Export data with formatting and layout. (This option is always turned on if you are exporting a form or a report.)

To open the destination Excel workbook once the export operation is finished, turn on the 'Open the destination file after the export operation is complete' check box.

Click OK.

If the export operation fails due to an error, Access displays a message that describes the cause of the error. Otherwise, Access exports the data and opens the destination workbook in Excel.

Importing or Linking to Data in Another Format

There are so many varieties of importing or linking with Microsoft Access that it isn't possible to cover them all (at least, not without writing a book entirely devoted to that subject). But here is a general list of the steps involved with importing or linking to other files:

Open the database that you want to import or link data into.

On the External Data tab, click the type of data that you want to import or link to. As an example, if the source data is stored in a Microsoft Excel workbook, click Excel.

In most cases, the Get External Data wizard will now appear. In the wizard, you may be asked for some or all of the following:

- The source location for the data

- Whether you want to import or link to the data

- When importing, whether to append the data to an existing table, or create a new table

- Precisely what data in the file should be imported or linked

- Whether the first row contains column headings, or whether it should be considered to be data.

- The data type of each column.

236

- Whether just the structure should be imported, or whether the structure and the data should be imported

- Whether Access should add a new primary key to any imported table, or use an existing key from the imported data.

- In the case of imports, a name for the new table

TIP: Before you export data from within Access, you may want to consider using a query as a source of the exported data. If you only want to make selected records or certain fields in the data available to the other program, creating and saving a query first, then basing the export on the query is often the easiest way to accomplish this task. To base the export on a query, you select the query in the navigation pane rather than choosing a table, then you choose your desired export options under the Export Data tab of the ribbon.

Summary

This chapter has provided you with a number of tips and techniques regarding sharing data between Microsoft Access and other software programs. Armed with this and other knowledge that you gained from the preceding chapters of this book, you should be well equipped to put Microsoft Access to effective use.

CONCLUSION (and a favor to ask!)

I truly hope that you enjoy learning about Microsoft Access 2013 as much as I have enjoyed writing about it. As an author, I'd love to ask a favor: if you've found my book to be helpful, please consider writing a short review. Your reviews help me to write better books. You can post a review by going to this book's page on the Amazon website (at www.amazon.com, search on the term 'microsoft access essentials 2013 edward jones'). Scroll to the bottom of the page, and click the 'Write a customer review' button at the lower left. And my sincere thanks for your time! (And to see additional books by this author, simply continue reading!)

-Ed Jones

Other books by the author: See the description of related technology titles on the next few pages. To visit the author's Amazon page for a complete list of books, go to the following web address and then click the Kindle Books link:

http://www.amazon.com/author/edwardjones_writer

Other books by the author include:

<u>Microsoft Word Fast and Easy</u>

If you're looking for a clear, well-written guide that will help you learn a maximum amount about Microsoft Word 2013, and spend a minimum amount of time doing so... you've come to the right place!

Microsoft Word 2013: Fast and Easy is THE book of "What you need to know" about the world's most popular word processor. In this comprehensive guide, you'll learn a variety of techniques that will help you quickly master this popular and powerful software. You will learn-

• How to get around within the user interface, and understand the major changes with the new Ribbon, tabs, and Backstage view

• How to use the new cloud-based features of Word 2013 to access your documents from multiple devices and multiple locations

• How to use your OneDrive cloud-based storage to share documents with others and collaborate with coworkers

• How to create documents that get your point across

• How to format your documents so their appearance demands respect

• How you can quickly create stunningly complex documents by taking advantage of templates

• How you can use Word's proofing tools to ensure that your documents contain no errors

With this book, you will learn just what you need to know to get the most out of Microsoft Word 2013!

Microsoft Excel 2013 Fast and Easy

You have better things to do with your precious time than to waste it, struggling to learn to use software! Learn everything that you need to know, and get the job done with the help of Microsoft Excel 2013: Fast and Easy!

If you're looking for a clear, well-written guide that will help you learn a maximum amount about Microsoft Excel 2013, and spend a minimum amount of time doing so... you've come to the right place!

Microsoft Excel 2013: Fast and Easy is THE book of "What you need to know" about the world's most popular spreadsheet. In this comprehensive guide, you'll learn a variety of techniques that will help you quickly master this popular and powerful software. You will learn-

• How to get around within the user interface, and understand the major changes with the Ribbon, tabs, and Backstage view

• How to use Microsoft OneDrive with Excel 2013 to store, access, and share workbooks from any computer or tablet with an internet connection

• How to create worksheets that get your point across

• How to format your worksheets so their appearance is a hit in the boardroom

• How you can quickly create stunningly complex worksheets by taking advantage of templates

• How you can use formulas and functions to provide the number-based results that YOU need

With this book, you will quickly learn what you need to know to get the most out of Microsoft Excel 2013!

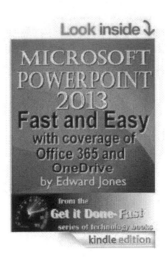

Microsoft PowerPoint 2013 Fast and Easy

If you've looked at the presentations shown by your competition (or even your co-workers), you already know that slide after slide of bullet points and a few charts just does not cut it anymore. And because it's YOUR reputation on the line... you've got to deliver a first-class presentation to that critical group of decision-makers, and you don't have time to waste struggling with obscure user manuals... this is the book that you need to get the job done right, and to get it done... FAST!

Microsoft PowerPoint 2013: Fast and Easy is THE book of "What you need to know" about the world's most popular presentation graphics software. Quickly learn what you need to know with this comprehensive guide to this popular and powerful program. You will learn-

• How to use the new cloud-based collaboration features of this version of PowerPoint to edit presentations simultaneously with others

• How to share presentations as e-mail links, as remote presentations "broadcast" over the web, and as posts on Facebook pages

• How to effectively navigate your way throughout the user interface, and understand the major changes with the new Ribbon, tabs, and Backstage view

• How to create presentations that go beyond "slides, bullet points, and charts"

• How to add transitions, audio, and video so the appearance of your presentation is a hit in the boardroom

• How you can quickly create slide shows that "pop" by taking advantage of templates and themes

• How you can include needed content from other software in your PowerPoint presentations

With PowerPoint 2013: Fast and Easy, you will learn 100% of all that you need to know to get the most out of Microsoft PowerPoint 2013!

Microsoft Access 2013 Essentials

**Print edition © 22 January 2015 by Jones-Mack
Technology Services of Charlotte, NC.**

The end.
(…yes, really!)

Printed in Great Britain
by Amazon